WHEN IT HURTS TO BE SINGLE

RANDY PETERSEN
AND ANITA PALMER

David C. Cook Publishing Co.
Elgin, Illinois—Weston, Ontario

David C. Cook Publishing Co.
Elgin, Illinois—Weston, Ontario
When It Hurts to Be Single

Published by David C. Cook Publishing Co.
850 N. Grove Ave., Elgin, IL 60120
Cable Address: DCCOOK
Designed by Christopher Patchel and Michael Letwenko
Illustrated by Michael Letwenko
Printed in the United States of America
Library of Congress Catalog Card Number: 88-70290

ISBN: 1-55513-883-7

CONTENTS

INTRODUCTION

BEING SINGLE IS NOT ITSELF A CRISIS. THERE ARE HUNDREDS of thousands of unmarried Christians who live happy and productive lives and would scorn the idea that their "state" is troublesome enough to be anywhere near a crisis.

Yet "Singles have many griefs and problems neither recognized nor understood by the rest of the world," writes Christian author Margaret Clarkson. "Many of us feel very much alone and overlooked in our churches, our needs for love and fellowship largely ignored."[1]

Many singles do at times feel as if they are in a hole. It may only be occasionally or it may be frequently, depending upon the maturity of the single person. A serious look around the average congregation will bear this out.

Tom is a 30-year-old single man, well-adjusted and successful—or so he seems. One day he discovers that his apartment building is being converted to condominiums; he must find a new place to live. Then, through no fault of his own, he loses his job. Next he discovers that his car's exhaust system is rusted out and needs to be replaced; he needs a root canal; and the woman he was dating and growing fond of has fallen in love with someone else.

What began as a simple though irritating inconvenience now has snowballed into a major identity crisis. Tom begins to wonder whether or not he'll be able to find another decent job. Every bill is a reminder of his perceived shortcomings. He also decides he's a loser when it comes to women, that he'll never get married. He can't sleep; he dreads getting up; he forgets to eat; he neglects his friends; he stops reading his Bible and praying.

Unemployment, car repair, and dental work are not unique to single people, of course. With a few changes, this could be the story of Joe and Betty, married people who live next door—except for one major difference. Tom goes through this alone. Joe and Betty have each other. Marriage does not cure all ills, but it does provide a certain equilibrium, a bracing, a sharing of the weight of life's problems.

What saves Tom from further plummeting to despair is an observant assistant pastor, who starts inviting Tom to breakfast every Tuesday morning. The pastor knows better than to assume Tom will "pull out of it" on his own, even though Tom looks like "a normal kind of guy." Tom needs help.

Sally, on the other hand, is a 34-year-old secretary with unexceptional looks and social skills. She does her job well and is well liked at the office, but goes home to an empty apartment at 5 p.m. She pops some popcorn and sits in front of the TV all evening, watching old movies and flipping through a copy of either *Virtue* magazine or *Cosmopolitan,* depending on how mad at God she is that night. As the movie's closing credits roll, she cries—half for the movie, half for herself. She is lonely. She longs for her Cary Grant to whisper those loving words to her, but knows the gap between her life and that screen-spun romance is ever widening.

The wife of an elder in her church notices that Sally is losing weight and looking sickly. She invites Sally over for dinner. Sally says no at first; it takes three or four invitations before she agrees. Dinner with the elder's family becomes a regular occurrence, the high point of Sally's week. But she still rides cycles of depression. At one point of particular crisis, the elder suggests that Sally see the church counselor for treatment.

This is a book for those who care about the Toms and Sallys in our churches and communities. It is a book for those who notice the lonely, the bitter, the hurting—those for whom singleness is a crisis—and want to help. It is a book for those who care about widows and widowers, the divorced, and people who have never married.

Perhaps you're a pastor or a Christian education director who has come to realize there is a portion of your congregation whose characteristics and needs are special—a subculture all its own, as one single pastor described it. Or perhaps you are a counselor without specific training in this area, and you've never helped a client whose self-described problem is "being single." Or maybe you're a friend of a hurting single person, and you want to know more about what she or he may be experiencing and how you can help.

Caring for singles in crisis is not easy. One problem is that this is a crisis without a name. That is, "singleness" doesn't really name the problem. Joe and Betty may reach the point where they plunk themselves down in a counselor's office and say, "Our marriage is on the rocks. Help us." But Tom and Sally are not likely to seek counseling on their own for "singleness." Yet their singleness may breed problems like depression, anxiety, withdrawal, feelings of inferiority, promiscuity, or anger.

Another complication is that many singles have no one to keep tabs on their mental and spiritual health. If Joe begins to show danger signs of a clinical depression, Betty will probably say, "It's time to get help." Who will say that for Tom or Sally? It takes the sensitive perception of that pastor or caring friend.

Still another obstacle is that the "cure" for singleness doesn't work—if the cure is marriage. Marriage changes the environment of the problems, but it may not change the problems. In fact, it is the mistaken belief that marriage will cure all ills that fosters many of the emotional problems of singleness. Sally puts off her personal growth until that future blessed day when she marries her knight in shining armor. She fears that she is not yet worthy of this blissful state. She may think God is punishing her by withholding this matrimonial "cure" for her loneliness.

This means that those who care for single people must be far more than matchmakers. They must show wisdom, patience, persistence, perception. "Effective helping requires far more than just gaining insights and skills," says mental health professional Paul Welter. "It involves on a deep level the kind of persons we are, and our willingness to invest time, energy, and sometimes suffering."[2]

Increasing one's effectiveness in ministry with all sorts of singles depends on deepening one's understanding of the full range of the singlehood experience. Thus this book begins with a look at the greater culture of which the church is a part. Following that, you'll find chapters on counseling ideas and case studies, as well as sample answers to questions many singles ask. A discussion of the theology of singleness and the theory behind singles ministry is also provided. For further study, turn to the annotated bibliography, where recommended books are listed.

Before we proceed, a few definitions are in order. We are including the divorced and widowed as we talk about "single" people. Obviously, their situations differ in many respects from those of the never married. But they share many of the traits and crises of all single people. We do not deal in depth with the specific problems of divorce or widowhood, since other books do that. Our focus is on areas of concern which are common to the broad range of single people.

A few thoughts about the word "single." Unfortunately the phrase "single people" has by usage shrunk to the noun "single." For example, "The singles' group is meeting tonight." "He's a single at First Baptist." This is a label that both aids communication and helps destroy it. Beth may have a Ph.D. in microbiology, manage a staff of 12, teach calligraphy on Thursday nights, and bake a mean apple pie. But to many, she's a "single," the only fact they can process. We prefer the noun phrase, if only to emphasize *"people."*

We, the authors, are not therapists. Our expertise in the matter of singleness comes from experience, as well as from interviews conducted with professional counselors. At this writing we are both single (never married) and in our early 30s. That gives us more than a score of years of adult single experience between us. That's a lot of TV dinners, lonely evenings, puzzling over the intricacies of dating relationships, and grappling with the temptations of the sexual revolution. Neither of us is a "confirmed" single person; that is, we both would like to be married people someday.

We have also observed singleness in our friends and colleagues. Both of us have been involved in church singles groups, either as leaders or participants. We have talked with our single friends over the years about singleness and have seen the joys and trials of the single life many times over.

Finally, we should say that we are both committed Christians. We believe in the church. It is our love for the church and our desire to see it minister as effectively as possible that leads us to bring you this helper's resource.

WHERE DO SINGLE PEOPLE HURT?

WHAT KIND OF WORLD DO SINGLE PEOPLE INHABIT? IF YOU believe what you read in the papers, it's a world tilted in their favor. The single life is free and easy. Single people have time to kill and money to burn. Or so the media images imply.

Live single for a while, however, and you find it "ain't necessarily so." The glorious image of the carefree single person fades under close scrutiny. Singleness *can* be fun, but those who lust after the reflection of the single life seen on the TV screen will go through life feeling they are missing something. Sadly, that's where many single people are—chasing bubbles that burst at a touch.

The Christian single person often feels the added tension of a church that doesn't quite know what to do with singleness. Though that situation is slowly changing, the Christian world in general has not done much to present an image of the *Christian* single life. So, if a Christian single person is chasing the bubbles blown by the secular media, he or she may feel that Christianity prevents the full attainment of that blissful single state. Some of these single people jump ship and chase that elusive image. Others stay on board as Christians, but resent God or the church for denying them the pleasures they see on TV.

How did this situation come to be? Let's examine this "world of singleness" and its origins more closely.

The Singleness Explosion

Singleness is on the rise. In the United States alone, the count has passed 60 million. Of Americans age 18 and over in 1984, 36.8 percent were single, according to U.S. Census figures.[1]

In 1984 nearly a quarter of all households in the U.S. (23 percent) consisted of only one person. The number of Americans living alone doubled between 1970 and 1985, climbing to 20.6 million.[2]

The number of single-parent families is also rising steadily. In 1986, 26.3 percent of all families with children in the U.S. were headed by a single parent. That's a staggering rise from 12.9 percent in 1970.[3]

You get the idea. The singleness boom is one of the major demographic trends of the last two decades.

That does not mean, however, that the percentage of single people has risen throughout history. In the 1960s and 1970s we were following a generation that had been unusually marriage minded. According to sociologists Leonard Cargan and Matthew Melko, the percentage of Americans 14 and older in 1979 who were single reached 40 percent—a steep climb from the 32.7 percent of 1960. But that was really a return to the levels of earlier decades. In 1940 the figure stood at 40.4 percent. In 1900, as many as 46 percent of adult Americans 14 and older were single.[4]

It is true that people are waiting longer to marry than they did a generation ago. In 1985, the median age for first marriages stood at 25.5 for men and 23.3 for women. In 1956 it was nearly three years younger, 22.5 for men and 20.1 for women. But go back to 1890 and today's figures look more normal; men married at 26.1 years on average, women at 22.[5]

In some ways, then, today's society should not be viewed as abnormally single. The 1940–1960 period could be considered "abnormally married." This is especially important for churches to note. Churches have tended to emphasize the nuclear family—mom, dad, and a few kids. With that approach, it is sometimes hard to find a place for single people. Yet that emphasis is not based on centuries of church tradition, but rather on one particularly marriage-minded generation. The church has always been "pro-family," but in previous generations it tended to widen the idea of "family" to include all kinds of relatives, as well as single friends.

So how should we read those population numbers? Is society becoming more "single" or not? Yes, the percentage of single people in our culture has risen markedly from a generation ago, but is returning to the levels of previous generations. Still, the increase is significant, perhaps unprecedented. Singleness is a growth industry.

For the church, that means greater opportunity to serve—if we understand single people and their needs.

Why the Boom?

There are significant cultural factors that have contributed to the boom in singleness. One is *the sexual revolution*.

This upheaval set our culture free to experiment with sex apart from marriage, sex for sex's sake. As Tim Stafford describes it, "The Sexual Revolution began, probably not because some free-thinkers wished it so, but simply because of penicillin and the Pill. The first could cure syphilis: sleeping around no longer meant risking your life. The second prevented babies, and thus suggested that sex's connection to the family was unnecessary. Sex could, for the first time in history, be separated from life-or-death consequences. Understandably, people's views of sex became more liberal, and so did their behavior."[6]

Suddenly, there was one less reason to get married—at least in the world's eyes. Sex was not reserved for marriage; it was an experience all its own. "Virgin" became a dirty word, applied only to "nerds" and "religious zealots."

The sexual revolution upended society's sense of right and wrong. As a result, more and more people decided to stay single. Being unmarried made it easier to carry on a life-style of sexual experimentation.

A second factor which seems to have contributed to the growth of the single population is *feminism*. Gone is the notion that a woman must be somebody's wife in order to "be somebody." Marriage once meant fulfillment for women—or so the promise went. Feminism challenged those assumptions, asserting the independence of women. Women began to prove that they could go it alone. Many of them have, choosing to "find themselves" as singles rather than "lose themselves" in a marriage.

A third cause of the singles boom is *divorce*. The increase in the divorce rate since 1960 has sent many scurrying back into singleness—some willingly, some not. The divorce increase is largely a product of the sexual revolution, liberalized divorce laws, and a consuming drive for comfort and self-fulfillment.

The divorce rate has climbed dramatically over the last quarter-century. Cargan and Melko show how the percentage of people in the U.S. who are divorced rose from 2.3 percent in 1960 to 5.2 percent in 1979.[7] U.S. Census Bureau figures from 1984 indicate that there were 12.2 million divorced people in the nation, representing 7.2 percent of the adult population.[8]

A fourth major cultural contributor to the growth in the number of single people is *The Me Generation*. American individualism may have reached its peak in the 1970s. It was every man for himself, every woman for herself; different strokes for different folks; do your own thing. It was *I'm OK and You're . . .* well, I don't spend much time thinking about you. Multitudes were seeking self-fulfillment, "finding themselves." That often meant a rejection of long-established social institutions—like marriage. So where does that leave us? With a huge social trend that encompasses millions of people. Unfortunately, the forces that brought about the singles explosion have proven fickle. They have not provided much support for those whose lives they have drastically affected.

Sexual Slavery

One force which has especially betrayed single people is the sexual revolution. It promised freedom, but has resulted in slavery. As Merle Shain observed in 1973, "Once we couldn't speak of sex and now we can't speak of love, and strangers go to bed together instead of shaking hands. But many of them don't like each other and still more don't like themselves, and impotence has replaced frigidity as the problem of the day. Women used to trade sex to get love and communication and sometimes they got it and sometimes they did not, so more of them are trading sex for sex itself these days, and because they are trading for goods and services they are trading sharper than before."[9]

In a substantial survey of the singles scene, Jacqueline Simenauer and David Carroll examined the attraction to singles bars. They describe it in terms of addiction. "They don't necessarily like singles bars, they don't really want to be there, but loneliness drives them on." A woman poignantly told them, "The foundation, walls and floor of the bar I go to are built of the same material: Hope." One man they interviewed finally "kicked the habit." He said, "I never went back to the bar, but, you know, I really had to fight the temptation several times. It was almost like trying to stop smoking."[10]

Jeffrey Ullman describes such a person as a "love junkie": "We become addicted to the overwhelming need to find someone, anyone, to be with."[11]

In *Love, Sex and the Single Man,* Aaron Hass echoes the cry of many:

The culture screams, "Enjoy casual sex. You are a man. Why get seriously involved or married anyway? All around you there are bitter divorce casualties and unhappily married people wishing they were single. Yet, here you are. Perhaps your work is not very satisfying. Maybe you are continually beset by economic pressures. Whatever your problems may be, you find it difficult to act happy all the time (as you feel you must in order to be successful in the singles world). And you're not really having that much fun. It is no surprise, therefore, that you and millions of other single men are asking, 'Is this all there is? Is this all I can hope for?' "[12]

The epidemic of AIDS (Acquired Immune Deficiency Syndrome) has seriously cramped the style of "swinging singles." Reports of the spread of that deadly, sexually transmitted disease among heterosexuals have made them more cautious about sexual experimentation. This has caused anxiety in many who are scared to death of contracting the virus, but feel unable to curtail their sexual liaisons.

This is the world single people live in, a world of promises that don't come true. Married people live there too, but they go home at night to the ripe old institution of marriage. The forces of sexual liberation, feminism, divorce, and individualism, have helped cause a singleness boom in our society. But those who choose being single, whether Christian or not, seldom find what was promised.

The Church Response

For many good reasons, Christians have opposed the forces of change that have brought about the boom in singleness: the sexual revolution, excessive feminism, divorce, selfish individualism. Singleness is viewed as a child of parents the church doesn't like; as a result, some Christians tend to pity single people, or suspect them. Single people, by their singleness, may be seen by some as rejecting marriage—another institution close to the church's heart.

But unless churches make a point of welcoming single people, accepting the cultural trend and ministering to people within it—as a number of churches are doing—single people will feel rejected, orphaned. That will make it even more difficult to meet the needs of single people who face crises.

Singleness is a major social trend. But it is more than that. It is a fact that touches people's lives deeply. All the statistics don't mean much to the woman who is crying because she is finally facing the truth that she will never marry and have children . . . or to the man who is struggling with the temptation to go to a singles bar and try to pick up a companion for the evening.

Will you help to bear the burdens of these people? Will you listen to them and show them the love of Christ? If so, the rest of this book can help you.

CHAPTER TWO

STAGES OF SINGLENESS: A KEY TO HELPING

WHEN YOU ARE HELPING A SINGLE PERSON, EITHER AS A friend or as a counselor, consider his or her *stage* of singleness. That may help you understand the person's needs more fully.

After all, single people come in different types and go through different experiences. Would it make sense to care for a 23 year old fresh out of college in the same way you would a 46 year old who has just failed in her third attempt at marriage? Of course not! Every individual should be dealt with individually.

One of the cardinal sins of counseling is "pigeonholing." That happens when you stop listening to the person as he or she relates specific, unique problems, and you assume that he or she fits into prototype A or B. People do fit into categories to some extent, but to stop listening is to become an ineffective helper. As long as you continue to listen to the person's description of his or her situation, you can and should compare that with helpful models and appropriate categories.

New Categories

The obvious categories of single people that come to mind are "old" and "young"; or "never married," "widowed," and "divorced." These are all valuable considerations, but we propose a different set of categories. These are based not on age or marital history, but on how one *feels* about one's singleness and whether one expects to *remain* single. Thus our attention is not on the past (how many years one has lived, whether one has married before), but on the present (how one feels now) and the future (whether one expects to be married someday).

Single people are either *voluntarily* or *involuntarily* single. And they expect to be either *temporarily* single or *permanently* so. There are fluctuations and degrees, of course. Some days, for example, Jeff is voluntarily single; he's glad to have the freedom to do what he wants. Other days he is involuntarily single; he feels lonely or neglected and wishes he were married. Thus he might be on the "cusp" of those two categories.

The temporary-permanent label is based on expectations, and these may change, too. Barbara, 35, is "permanent" when she comes to grips with the thought that she probably will not marry. But when she meets and begins to date a man she really likes, her expectations suddenly change. She reverts to the "temporary" category.

Simply put, we have four types of people represented here, each saying a different thing about singleness:

Voluntary temporary: "I probably will marry someday, but I'm happy being single."

Involuntary temporary: "I probably will marry, and I hope it's soon, because I don't like being single."

Voluntary permanent: "I probably will never marry, and that's fine, because I like being single."

Involuntary permanent: "I probably will never marry, and I don't like that at all."

Let's take a closer look at the kind of person you're likely to meet in each of these categories.

Voluntary Temporary

Voluntary temporaries tend to be young—18-30. They come out of college or high school and play the "singles scene" for a few years before marrying. At least that's usually their plan. What they look for in a church singles group is fun, friends, and maybe some dates.

Voluntary temporaries sometimes face difficulty in adjusting from college or high school life to single life; their crew of school friends is gone and they have no support network. Often they have serious questions about their work. What field should they go into? How important should work be in their lives? What sort of ethical decisions must they make on the job? And of course there are often problems with sex. The world keeps telling these young adults that sex is natural and easy and there for the taking.

In many cases, these single people are newly freed from the constraints of parental rules. They are, for the first time in their lives, in a position to consider the world's claims and act on them. Single people in this stage often need to evaluate rules already learned and make them their own—or make *up* their own.

Counselor Wayne Eastlack says, "I find people going through times of questioning more in their 20s than in other times. It's a time of values clarification, where they take a critical look at what they were taught. It is a tumultuous time for many, but I think it can be healthy."

Eastlack adds that anxiety disorders may crop up during this time, caused by identity confusion and high expectations. Just when these single people are wondering who they are, what they believe, and what they should do with their lives, a multitude surrounds them, saying, "You have such potential. We expect great things of you—if you don't blow it." It's the same sort of identity confusion teenagers often face, but with a double dose of expectations.

In fact, this period can resemble a teenage rebellion—deferred a few years. But the bonds have been burst; the single person has that long-craved freedom. What will she or he do with it? Often church involvement is not high on the "things to do" list, which can diminish the influence of the church on the lives of voluntary temporaries.

One 26-year-old single woman told us: "I miss the group of people we had in college. I wish there was a bunch of people around here who would just do stuff together. I'm not looking for dates. I just want a group of girlfriends and guy friends to do things with."

An active singles group would do wonders for this woman, and she was shopping around for one. Some single people can do their own networking, but it's not easy when you don't know anyone in your area. Some of the best "ministers" to single people we have known have been those who made connections for them. Often these helpers are older, married Christians who just have a knack for introducing people: "Oh, do you know so-and-so? You should! He's interested in the same kind of thing." At this point we're not talking about matchmaking, but friend making.

Sometimes the voluntary temporary gets tired of the casual friendships and longs for a deeper (but not necessarily romantic) relationship. This is a second basic need that Christians can offer to meet. This cannot be forced, but deep friendships are so desperately needed in the lives of some single people that a little extra effort by the helper in that direction couldn't hurt.

In her book, *The Joy of Being Single,* Janice Harayda presents a "job description" of a friend. Friends keep secrets, she says. They show loyalty, sticking up for each other. They praise each other, offering criticism when it's really necessary—but are mostly affirming. Friends fuss over each other's hurts, caring for each other when they're sick. They help each other move, honor each other on their big days—birthdays, promotions, etc.—and touch each other. They return telephone calls, give shelter, give gifts. These simple expressions of friendship are lacking in many single people's lives.

When dealing with the emotional problems of voluntary temporaries, be wary of that potential double whammy of identity crisis and high expectations. Without minimizing the current crisis, let the person know that it is not unusual for people in that situation to experience anxiety. That message, if the person receives it, may keep him or her from further anxiety.

Avoid adding to the person's expectations. It doesn't help to assure that someday he or she will find the perfect spouse, be phenomenally successful at business, or go on to help others through similar crises. That just adds pressure. Affirm the person in the present: "You look good, you're fun to be with, I enjoy our friendship." Offer your unconditional love: "No matter what you do in the future, I will be your friend."

Spiritual crises add a new dimension to the problems of young single people. As they evaluate their beliefs, they often test new life-styles. A story is told of the great preacher Donald Grey Barnhouse, who spoke at a certain college campus in the 1950s. Afterward a young woman told him, "I don't believe the Bible anymore. I just don't see how that could be true."

Barnhouse looked right at her and said, in effect, "You're living in sin, aren't you?" She confessed that she and her boyfriend had been sinning sexually and that had drawn her away from the Lord.

Barnhouse was presuming a lot, but he knew that beliefs and behavior are deeply connected. When we are tempted to sin, the next temptation is to change our beliefs to "allow" the sin. You don't need to be as confrontational as Barnhouse was, but you could alert the young adult to this tendency. Remember, though, that doctrinal questioning is not necessarily an indication of behavioral sin.

Involuntary Temporary

The second group of single people consists of *involuntary temporaries*. They want and expect to get married. These tend to be older, in their late 20s or 30s. In many cases, they have "done" the singles scene as voluntary temporaries and are tired of it.

Potential problems include the lack of communication with other single people, or miscommunication. For example, one person who wants marriage may be dating another who just wants to have fun. In such a case, the marriage-minded person may be frustrated.

Some older single people in this category distance themselves from younger single people because of the age difference and lack of common interests. This limits their opportunities to find marriage partners. In addition, involuntary temporaries often isolate themselves by rejecting "mere" friendships in pursuit of their romantic ideal.

Loneliness and boredom are common problems for those in this category, though that is often tempered by a certain comfortable familiarity with single life. Often such people experience the conflict of wanting the intimacy of married life, but not wanting to give up their independent ways.

Good church singles groups with a broad range of people can meet many of the needs of involuntary temporaries. Individual Christians can reach out in simple friendship to those in this category, who are more apt to receive it than some voluntary temporaries are.

Caring people can also minister to this group through prudent matchmaking. There are certainly many pitfalls in trying to "fix someone up" or arrange blind dates, and matchmaking is too often attempted by those who are not genuine friends. For true friends, the rules are (1) Communicate with everyone involved; (2) Don't push; (3) Give both parties an easy out; and (4) Get out of the way.

Voluntary Permanent

The next category includes those who don't expect to get married and feel good about that—the *voluntary permanents*. These are usually well-adjusted people, spiritually and emotionally. They have gone through some crises, perhaps, but are secure in their singleness. These are usually older than the temporaries, about 35 and up. In many cases they are active in their churches or in some other form of Christian service.

There are not many voluntary permanents. Studies show that only five percent of never-married single people are "confirmed" in their singleness. Adding widows and divorced people might increase that percentage slightly, but this is still a small minority.

That fact can make voluntary permanents feel odd, abnormal, left out. Despite the fact that there are more single people than ever, most of them plan to get married someday, and *will* get married. They may be waiting longer to marry, they may be fresh out of school, they may be between marriages; but they are headed for marriage. Not so for the permanent singles.

Voluntary permanent singles need to be included in the church, befriended by church people, and employed in church service. Too often they are shunted into a singles group with a band of young temporaries with whom they have little in common. Churches need confirmed single people in the fabric of their fellowships.

Church programs can't do it all, of course. Individual Christians need to reach out in friendship to permanent singles, and will often find it rewarding to do so. While befriending younger, temporary singles can be a difficult and sometimes one-way effort, friendships with older singles is usually well-received and warmly reciprocated. Church couples can play "surrogate parent" to younger singles, but the older ones need brothers and sisters. Invite them over, and let them invite you over. Let them give you as much as you give them.

Involuntary Permanent

The fourth category consists of those who doubt that they will ever marry and are not happy with that. These are the *involuntary permanents,* and they tend to exhibit the most emotional and spiritual problems. They have not "made their peace" with singleness. They tend to be mad at God, and mad at the world for ignoring their need to marry. Often they are mad at themselves, or feel that they are utter failures because they have not married.

Ministry to involuntary permanents involves moving them into the "voluntary" category—helping them to accept their singleness and find some contentment there. It is generally not ideal to group these people with younger, temporary singles; that may just make them feel more out of place. Involuntary permanents need to be included in the entire church life. They need to be encouraged and "adopted" (as brothers and sisters, not surrogate children) by church families.

Of all singles, people in this category most often go to counselors with their problems. Laypeople need to recognize that the serious problems exhibited by some in this group may require professional help.

As with the temporaries, there is a "cusp" between voluntary and involuntary. For some, accepting one's singleness is a constant struggle. One day 33-year-old Deanna is doing fine; then she goes to a wedding or a church supper and suddenly feels mad at God again. Or a close friend gets married and Deanna feels "betrayed."

Even the most well-adjusted single people experience occasional times of rank dissatisfaction with their singleness. This is normal, nothing to worry about—though it may require some care and prayer.

Progressing Through the Stages

How do people progress through these categories? Are there transition points that demand special attention? How can caring Christians be alert to these potential crisis times?

Most people enter the single world as voluntary temporaries. ("Entering the single world" is an odd concept, since we are all born single—but we are speaking of the entry into adult single life.) For most people in our culture this occurs after graduation from high school or college. Some start off as involuntary temporaries, wanting to get married as soon as possible. A few devote themselves to ministry as singles from the start or consider themselves unmarriageable; these would enter on the permanent side. But generally people "enter" singleness as voluntary temporaries.

For most, there is at least a brief move into "involuntary temporary" before leaving the single world and getting married. That is, at some point they decide marriage is better than singleness, even if they have not been actively seeking a mate. For our purposes we'll speak of involuntary temporaries as those who have no particular mate in mind when they become "involuntary." They decide they want to get married, not because marriage to a particular man or woman is so appealing, but because they are tired of being single.

Most voluntary temporaries get married. Their expectations—that they will get married—prove correct. But some don't. They revise their expectations. The years pass and, for whatever reasons, they are still single. They begin to think, *Maybe I was wrong. Maybe I will never marry.* When they cross the "line" and become 60 or 70 percent sure that they *won't* get married, they move to the "permanent" side.

Some of the involuntary permanents learn to cope well with their singleness. They become voluntary permanents. Others remain involuntary permanents, often growing bitter or sullen.

That is the general progression. But there is some backward movement. Certain things can happen to a well-adjusted voluntary permanent to make him or her regress into involuntary status and become bitter. A "permanent" may suddenly meet the "right" person and be swept back to the temporary side—expecting that he or she will get married. An involuntary temporary might change his or her mind and decide it's okay to be single after all.

We must also consider reentry into the single world. Divorced and widowed people figure into the categories, too. Those who instigate divorces would tend to be on the voluntary side; they have chosen to become single. Victims of divorce tend to be on the involuntary side. Widows and widowers would tend to enter on the involuntary side and, as they deal with their bereavement, move toward the voluntary.

Crisis Points and the Stages

Certain crisis points in the lives of all of us—the "mid-life crisis," for instance—are well-known. At these times in our personal development we are especially susceptible or needy. Sometimes we can turn that need into an exciting, new direction. Are there similar crisis points in the progression of single people?

We suggest that there are four such turning points that need attention from anyone serious about caring for single people. These are the major movements through the categories of single life:

1. *Entry to single life*. The first year after college or high school (or divorce or the death of a spouse) is crucial. There we

find loneliness and longing for old times as well as experimentation with new life-styles.

2. *When voluntary temporary singleness becomes involuntary.* This transition usually happens slowly. The person grows dissatisfied with the single life. This can be accompanied by cynicism, complacency, laziness, and lack of direction. The person needs coaching, encouragement, and grounding in Biblical priorities.

3. *When temporary singleness becomes permanent.* The person finally gives in to the probability that he or she will probably never marry. This can be a jolting time of revamping one's dreams, plans, and purposes in life. Such a person needs help to find new channels for the energy previously expended on those dreams and plans. He or she needs to remember the calling of God, that we are here to please Him as *He* chooses.

4. *When voluntary permanent singleness flits back to involuntary.* Some incident, or a collection of them, can trigger dissatisfaction in the most well-adjusted person. Lovingly, friends and other helpers should ease the person back into acceptance.

These stages of singleness are not a magic formula. But they may help you to understand where single people are on their personal journeys through life, and to prepare to guide them through the rocky places.

CHAPTER THREE

COUNSELING SINGLE PEOPLE

"THIS IS SILLY. I SHOULD BE ABLE TO DEAL WITH THIS problem myself," says Jill, a 29-year-old single woman, as she takes a seat in her pastor's office.

So goes the attitude of many single people. They need help, but are too embarrassed to seek it. The world's image of the suave single, coolly handling whatever life dishes out, doesn't help matters. Single people also lack the support of a spouse who says, "Go get help."

If it is difficult for single people to talk to you about their problems, they won't do it. That's why you need to make it as easy as possible by being approachable. Pastors, counselors, and even friends need to let people know when they're available and how to set up a meeting. Helpers should telegraph their willingness to help.

Single people on the fringes of church life sometimes think, "The pastor's too busy to be bothered with my problem," or, "I'm not involved enough in the church for the pastor to care about me." Pastors and church counselors can overcome these assumptions by openly declaring their availability. In Jill's case, the pastor followed up a "How are you?" at the church door with a deeper inquiry—and invited her to come and talk with him if she wanted to.

Close friends of single people can go a step further. They should look for warning signs in the lives of their single friends: trouble eating or sleeping, nervousness, a chronically negative outlook, withdrawal, sudden changes in life-style or attitude. A simple "Do you want to talk about it?" may be the first step in a healing process. There is a fine line between being concerned and being intrusive, so tread lightly; but since the single person has no spouse to act as monitor, that task is left to his or her closest friends.

Whether you're a friend, pastor, or counselor, the following principles should be useful as you seek to help hurting single people.

The Presenting Problem

In a nonthreatening way, the helper needs to start the counseling with a question: "Why are you here?" Regardless of how the question is worded, it gives the single person a chance to define the "presenting" problem, the trouble that brought him or her there. If the counselor is a friend who has spotted a problem and mentioned it, the question may be, "What's going on? Why are you acting so strange?" Jill's pastor asks her, "What *is* the problem?"

The person doesn't need to *analyze* the problem now; that will come later. He or she should simply state the concrete aspects of the situation. You could help with questions like, "How do you feel? Lonely? Sad? Guilty? Are you doing things you don't want to do? Do you have questions that are bothering you? Are you having trouble making decisions?"

As Jill begins, she says, "The problem is that I'm 35 years old and not married." That's not really the problem; that's an analysis of the problem, and probably not a good one. Jill's pastor doesn't say this; he doesn't want to scare her off. He directs her into a more concrete description: "How do you feel about that?"

He's looking for an answer like, "I want very much to be married," "I feel lonely," or "I'm afraid I will never amount to anything." These are all better statements of the presenting problem.

"I feel very sad about that," says Jill. "I feel like I'm missing out on life."

The Initial Response

Coming to a counselor and stating a problem, or opening up to a church leader or friend, is very threatening to most single people. He or she is revealing a very intimate part of himself or herself, and doesn't know whether you will applaud or ridicule. The person has let down his or her armor and now stands vulnerable to your harming or healing touch.

Jill still isn't sure exactly what motivated her to see the pastor. She had been feeling very depressed and thought his kindness might help. But sitting in his office she feels like a patient, a sick person, and she doesn't like that image of herself.

The single person is especially vulnerable in such situations because he or she is probably not used to such intimacy. Some single people are good at opening up to others, but many are afraid of this, or at least unpracticed at it. For some, the fear of intimacy may have kept them single. If they have reached the point where they decide to share their crisis with a counselor, they find themselves in uncharted territory.

Once the problem has been stated, affirmation is in order. Help the person feel at ease by communicating that (1) it is okay to have problems; and (2) it is good to seek help. That is not to say that the problems are okay. If a single man confesses that he has been sleeping with a different woman each week and can't stop, you can't tell him his behavior is okay. But the problem is not unheard of, and it is fixable. His compulsion is not a terminal disease. He has already chosen the road to recovery by coming to you for help.

Affirmation can be difficult, especially if the problem comes as a surprise. The first reaction of the pastor who hears of this single man's promiscuity may be severe disappointment. Yet the pastor can be glad the man has come for help, and should affirm him for that.

Would-be helpers may be tempted to make light of certain problems: "Lonely? That's silly, with all these people around." Unfortunately, the single person probably already thinks the problem is silly—that "normal" people deal with these things on their own—and the statement just reinforces that. Take time to acknowledge that the trouble is real, at least real enough for the person to share it with you. After some mutual searching, you may both conclude that the problem *is* less serious than the person thought, and that it can be easily dealt with. But in any case the initial response should show acceptance, affirmation, and support.

"Well, I'm glad you have come," says Jill's pastor. "A lot of people—even married people—have that sense of 'missing out on life,' and they don't know what to do about it. Maybe we can start finding some answers."

Assess the Urgency of the Problem

In *How to Help a Friend,* psychologist Paul Welter discusses five levels of urgency along with the sort of help a lay counselor might need to provide:[1]

1. *Problem.* Welter defines a problem as a situation in which there is a solution. As a counselor, you don't need to get too

involved personally, and your advice meets little resistance.

For instance, your friend Ann is unhappy in your church. In a conversation after Sunday School she asks whether you think it would be wrong for her to start visiting other congregations to see whether there are any singles groups in the county.

Once you understand the specific nature of the problem and the help being asked for, you can provide information if you have it—or find it if you don't.

2. *Predicament.* In a predicament there is no easy or satisfactory solution. The person will have a feeling of being trapped, though there is not a sense of great urgency. It is important for the helper to get involved: to talk with the person, listen to him or her, do activities together.

Ann is now in a predicament. She has talked to a church elder during the week; he told her that "church shopping" is wrong, that she must pray that God will change her attitude. She tells you that she's on the verge of losing her job, so she may be moving anyway—and besides, she says, no one would notice when she left. You know she has no family in the area.

Welter advises avoiding giving advice, at least at first, when helping a person in a predicament. Instead, work for "openness" rather than "closure"; show respect; be concrete.

3. *Crisis.* A crisis, writes Welter, is "a short-term predicament in huge proportions." In a crisis there is definitely an urgency. A person in crisis may exhibit a number of these characteristics: not listening or responding; not looking at you; seeming caught up in thought; not acting characteristically; not getting along with those who are usually close; and not concentrating on work.

It has been two weeks since you last talked to Ann. You catch sight of her on the edge of the crowd leaving church and say hello. She looks distracted, then tells you that her boss indeed fired her, that her savings are depleted due to recent surgery, and that her rent is due on Friday. When you ask whether she is worried about meeting the deadline, she mutters something to herself and walks away.

Welter says that in a crisis it is important to take time to be with the victim. Establish eye contact; touch the person if appropriate; bring him or her into the present. Walk alongside the person emotionally rather than leaping ahead to find a solution. Accept the person's point of view as true for him or her, but be willing to state another. Suggest church or community resources. It is usually at this point that a professional counselor or pastor is consulted—or should be.

"Look for emotional indicators which will let you know whether your friend is emerging from the crisis or moving into it," writes Welter. "If the person is not able to resolve the crisis, then he may move into a panic situation. It is necessary that there be at least one person who says to the one who is in a state of crisis, 'If you need me, just call me anytime.'"

4. *Panic*. Welter calls this "the wild flight." It usually lasts minutes, but may last for hours. People in panic are frightened ("afraid of a dreadful threat to their immediate future"). They will "run," either actually or mentally, though their appearance may remain relatively calm. Often they feel there is only one way out.

Ann is at the panic stage. She is on the phone, nearly hysterical. Her landlord has just told her he is going to evict her.

Now is the time to call attention to the present relationship between you and the victim; get in touch with him or her through eye contact, touch, verbal assurance. Then work with him or her as you would with a person in crisis.

Follow-up is important. Writes Welter, "There needs to be a person who remains there for support so that the person does not move back into a state of panic. . . . This is especially true at night when there are fewer helping persons and agencies available."

5. *Shock*. This is "the dazed walk," according to Welter, in which there is no recognition reflex, no true dialogue. The person has no ability to recall the immediate past; all emotions are shut down.

You arrive at Ann's apartment and find her on her front doorstep, surrounded by all her furniture. She has just discovered that her belongings were thrust out while she was gone. She says nothing, just stares at the notice she's holding.

When aiding a person in this stage, you must be confident. Expect to help; get close. Show respect and work slowly. Don't be alarmed if the person suddenly becomes active. And don't assume the shock is only psychological (in some cases, it could be diabetes or medicine, etc.). Stay with the person until he or she comes out of it.

Most of the "singles in crisis" this book is concerned with

will fall into the middle three categories. Many have easily solvable problems, but they would often work these out themselves without seeking help. Singleness may be described as a predicament for some, an environment in which various problems may fester with no easy solution. For some it will reach a point of crisis, including periods of severe depression or loneliness. The breakup of a romance or the departure of close friends, for instance, may result in a crisis of rejection. On occasion, single people may experience times of panic in which they just have to talk with somebody—when they are so lonely they feel they are going out of their minds.

Let's return to the example of Jill, the young woman who came to her pastor with a "silly" problem. The pastor needs to probe further to assess Jill's need. He asks a few questions about her current situation, not about its causes or background.

Pastor: Are there times when you get so sad about this that you just can't do anything?

Jill: How did you know? Yes. I almost didn't come here today. That's why I was a little late. I just stood at the door with my coat on and wondered whether I should call and say that I was sick.

Pastor: Any other times that happens?

Jill: Sometimes at night I'll get home from work and . . . well, I'll wish I was married. I fix myself something to eat and start thinking about what it would be like to fix that meal for a husband. So then I usually start to cry. So I take my dinner and sit in front of the TV until it gets late. Sometimes the dinner doesn't even get eaten. I throw it out and then go to bed.

Pastor: Have you had any trouble eating or sleeping?

Jill: Not sleeping. I've always slept like a log. Eating? Well, I go on binges. Sometimes I'll feel so sorry for myself I eat everything in the kitchen. Then I get mad at myself and decide to diet. After all, what guy's going to want me if I'm fat? But after a couple of days I figure, "What's the use?" and pig out again. I guess that's pretty weird, isn't it?

Pastor: Not really. You'd be surprised how many people do that very thing. Tell me, how are your feelings affecting your relationships with other people?

Jill: Not too much, I think. I get along pretty well with people.

Pastor: Any particular relationships where your singleness is a problem?

Jill: Well, with Sheila and Bob. She was my old roommate. We were very close. But then she got married to Bob a couple of years ago. I still see them a lot. They have a baby now—Jeremy—so I baby-sit sometimes and do other stuff with them.

Lately . . . I don't know . . . Sheila's been getting on my nerves. She just doesn't seem to be a very good mother or wife. And once in a while I think how wrong it is that she has all this and doesn't know what to do with it, and I'd be so good at it, but I'm all alone.

Pastor: How does that make you feel?

Jill: Angry sometimes. And sad. I come home from their place all worn out. Sometimes I think what it would be like if I were married to Bob.

Pastor: Are these sexual fantasies?

Jill (embarrassed) : Not—not really. Just, you know, nice. It's just stuff I think about.

Pastor: How are you feeling about God these days?

Jill: Oh, He's wonderful. Really. I have some questions for Him, though.

Pastor: Like what?

Jill: Where's He hiding my man?

From his questioning, the pastor guesses that Jill is probably at the predicament level, but may be veering into crisis. She seems fairly well-adjusted, but those binges of eating, as well as her inaction and indecision, could get worse.

Knowing Your Limits

When a person enters the crisis stage and beyond, it's usually time for the lay counselor to give way to the professional. A friend can still give support, but should urge the troubled person to see a trained counselor, even to the point of finding the number and handing the person a phone. Another limit to recognize has to do with personal attachments. Sometimes you will not be the right person to counsel a crisis victim who is single. The young woman who keeps falling in love with father-figures should probably not spend a lot of time in the pastor's office, for example. A woman who just broke up with a man may want to help him through his crisis of rejection, but she would probably only hurt him more. Even psychologists encounter times when patients develop unhealthy dependence and ought to be referred elsewhere.

Be sensitive to sexual and romantic complications in the counseling process. Single people are especially susceptible; some have a tendency to see everything in romantic terms. For some hurting women, a male counselor may be the only man who has ever cared about them; they may not know how to handle it. Show concern, but keep things professional. If you begin to sense a problem, talk about it and set the bounds of the counseling relationship.

Jill's pastor has already observed a limit in his session with her. When he asked about sexual fantasies she got nervous about it, so he changed the subject. He may guess that she has indulged in sexual fantasies and felt some guilt about that. She may even be fighting a private battle with lust. These might be important conflicts to deal with, but the pastor knows he is not the one to do so. He has known Jill since she was seven, has known her family, and is too close for Jill to share these private things with. If he suspects that these are major problems, and that she will never feel comfortable talking about them with him, he may refer her to another counselor.

Find the Person's Living Channels

Paul Welter writes of four "living channels": feeling ("awareness of one's emotions, and the ability to express them"), thinking ("the ability to plan and the ability to connect cause and effect"), choosing ("establishing a clear set of values and moral standards, finding meaning in life and having the courage or will to act"), and doing ("performing whatever action is desired or necessary").[2]

Welter believes that "usually we have a wide channel or two and a narrow channel or two." A person who has a strong choosing channel for instance, tends to be courageous and to have a clear value structure. "The person who has a constricted choosing channel," on the other hand, "is indecisive because (1) he lacks the courage to make a decision on insufficient evidences (and the evidences are always insufficient); or (2) . . . he does not have a value structure that is well organized. If all his values are equally important to him there is no way for him to prioritize in order to make a decision."

Welter concludes, "To the extent that all four of the channels are open and strong, our lifestyle is rich and fulfilling."

Jill, for instance, shows a strong thinking channel. She is bright, already figuring out some aspects of her predicament. Her weak channels are choosing and feeling. She stands at the door and can't decide whether to go for counseling or not; she sits in front of the TV and can't choose to eat her dinner; she feels sad, jealous of her close friend, and, it appears, has trouble controlling her feelings.

Healing for Jill will mean that she will feel better about her singleness and that she will be empowered to make choices. For someone with a weak thinking channel—say, someone who misinterprets events to mean that no one likes him or her—the therapy goal is to get him or her to *know* better what is going on, to see reality and piece it together more accurately. For someone with a weak doing channel—say the man who can't seem to break the habit of sleeping around—the goal is a change in behavior.

Feelings, Values, Actions

So far the counselee's problem has been stated and the initial appraisal made. This may all happen in the first session. Now begins the process of digging into the problem, to see more clearly what it is, where it came from, and what to do about it.

As the pastor counsels Jill, he discovers that much of her bad feeling is rooted in faulty assumptions. She feels she is not worth very much because no one has married her. Having grown up with the idea that marriage is a reward for being good and beautiful, and with no reward by age 35, she concludes that she must be bad and ugly.

Jill has also assumed that her purpose in life is to be a good wife to some good man. Her mother always told her that she would make a great wife, and trained her in the "necessary" domestic duties. If Jill never marries then, she will never fulfill her purpose. So where is the meaning in life?

This "What's the use?" attitude hinders Jill's decision making. *Does it matter if I eat this or not? Does it matter if I get fat? Does it matter if I just stare at the TV? Does it matter if I go for counseling?* If nothing matters, how can Jill make choices?

It is not easy to alter one's assumptions, and Jill has 35 years of ingrained attitudes. But she does have a strong thinking channel. She does see the link between her ideas and her feelings and choices, and she should be able to talk herself into some improvement.

Sometimes actions as well as attitudes can cause problems. A single man, for example, may feel lonely because he is always shying away from people—or because he is unknowingly giving off signals that say, "I want to be alone." Values may also cause trouble. This is particularly true among Christians who have learned to favor others over themselves. As a value this is good, but some have taken it to a point at which they don't care for themselves at all. They feel bad about themselves, they think ill of themselves, and do things that hurt themselves.

Likewise, feelings may affect the person's ability to cope. Many with weak thinking channels base their assumptions on their feelings—"This feels right to me, so it must be true." Many base their choices on what feels good to them. But what if they feel bad? Then they may assume God doesn't like them; they lose their desire to choose ("What's the use?"); and they try to relieve the bad feelings in the short term with actions (like eating everything in the kitchen) that often make them feel worse overall.

As a counselor, then, examine:

- Assumptions ("What do you think about this? Why does this make sense to you? Is this the way things really are?")
- Emotions ("How do you feel about this? Do you like it, not like it? How deeply do you feel about this?")
- Values ("Which is more important to you, this or that? Why is this more important? Is this right or wrong? If you could do such and such, would you?")
- Actions ("What do you do when you're by yourself? When you're with people? How do others seem to react?")

Watch for Self-Image Problems

One counselor told us that virtually all of the single people he sees have self-image problems at the roots of their crises. They can't cope with the world because they can't cope with themselves. This may emerge in ways like these:

- Self-hate: ("I don't like myself. I can't stand being alone because I drive myself crazy." "I hate myself when I'm with others.")
- Self-deprecation: ("I'm not very good at anything. I have nothing to offer anyone else.")

- Self-denial: ("I shouldn't do anything to please myself. That would be indulgent. Others always come first.")
- Self-destruction: ("I indulge in activities that hurt or humiliate me—drugs, alcohol, wild sexual behavior.")

Jill, for instance, may be showing a little of all these, though self-deprecation seems to be the main problem. She assumes that, since she is not married, she must not be any good.

Singleness often worsens self-image problems. Marriage is not always affirming, but many spouses help their mates toward a realistic appraisal of themselves. Single people often lack that outside perspective. They have to find it in close, honest friends—a precious commodity—and may begin to downgrade themselves if left to their own devices.

The counselor needs to affirm the single person, and to do so realistically. Psychologist Paul Keating says, "One of the roles we play as counselors is that of a mirror. We hold up a mirror and say, 'That's the way it looks to me. How do you see it?' "Then they can agree or deny. They may say, 'No, that's not the way I see it at all,' but it's still healthy to get someone else's opinion." The counselor calls the patient to see reality, saying, in effect, "You are not really as bad as you think you are."

Married people can generally say, "My spouse has chosen to be with me and accept me. Maybe I should accept myself." Single people, even popular ones, often have problems of self-hate. They sometimes feel that no one knows the real person inside, and would find that "real" self despicable. Married people can feel this way, too, but many have spouses whose presence says, "I know you intimately, and I'm still here."

A person suffering from self-hate will probably assume you don't like him or her very much. Within the bounds of your counseling, pastoral, or friend relationship, convey your appreciation for the person. Then search for the roots of the self-hate and analyze them. You may want to urge the person into comfortable social situations in which others will be affirming as well.

As for self-denial, we *should* put others first. The concept of "looking out for number one" is the world's idea, not that of Jesus, who sacrificed Himself on our behalf. But even Jesus took time out to rest; He went to parties and enjoyed the company of good friends. He said, "Love your neighbor as yourself" (Mt. 19:19).

Some single people, partly because they have never learned to receive by interacting with a spouse, feel guilty for any act of self-preservation or self-pampering. They need a helper to give them permission to do something for themselves. Psychologist Scott Schafer says, "People come to a counselor for permission, power, and protection. They often know what to do, but they need to be told it's okay. They need a pep talk and assurance that it will be all right." They can then do something good for themselves, because "My shrink told me to."

Self-destruction occurs most easily in solitude. Many married people hurt themselves with drink or drugs, but often have spouses who can blow the whistle. Single people, especially those living alone, can begin the descent into destructive behavior without anyone knowing it. By the time someone does discover it, it may be too late.

One 30-year-old businessman, a new Christian, suffered a divorce and a broken engagement. An emotional dependent, he sparked those breakups by being too demanding. He was also an alcoholic, but denied it. His counselor tried to get him out of the after-work drink pattern and into a church singles group—but had only moderate success.

Says that man's counselor, "The wish for fulfillment and the wish for self-destruction play themselves out in many people's experiences. [This man] could be a success in anything he does, but he's being very self-destructive because success is distressing to him.

"The process of restructuring one's behavior patterns is very difficult. A person really needs a coach or mentor, because people can seldom do this on their own. When the church is functioning at its best, it can provide some of these support systems. One of the things being talked about currently is 'Christian mentoring,' where older Christians are available to younger people as they are struggling through some of these developmental experiences. That's an idea as old as Paul and Timothy, but it could be helpful in many of these situations."

Hunt Down the Historical Roots

It's all fine to say to a self-hating patient, "But God loves you." Yet that person may not be able to grasp that thought until he or she scuttles some old baggage. It may be some event, or a comment from a classmate or sibling or parent.

Much has been made of counseling as detective work, with the detective-psychologist searching out clues from the patient's deep, dark history. But these clues are often less for the counselor and more for the patient. "It helps them to know how they got into this mess, because now they know how they can get out," says psychologist Wayne Eastlack.

Jill's idea that "I am no good unless I marry" is not some infallible Scriptural truth. It was an idea she derived from her well-meaning mother, and the derivation was wrong. Now Jill can set about changing her mind. That process is not easy, because the mistaken assumption is like a crease once ironed into a pair of pants, and ironed again and again for 20 years. It will take work to change that, but it is possible.

It is not always necessary to delve into a person's past, but you can often unearth helpful information with questions like these:

- When do you first remember feeling this way? Can you tell me about that situation?
- Why do you think that? Is that something you learned from your parents? From your friends? From school?
- Why is this so important to you? Have you had to make such choices in the past? What were the results?
- How long have you been doing this? When did you first do this? What do you remember about that?

Look for Answers

"The basis of counseling is not: You give the problem, I'll give the answer," says psychologist Keating. "They already know the answer; you have to help them find it." Your perceptive questions may dig out the evidence single people need to put things together for themselves.

As you listen, you may develop theories about the causes of the person's trouble. Present these, but as suggestions. Not, "Your problem seems to be . . . ," but, "Could it be that. . . ?" Let the person work with you on that hunch.

Don't make decisions for the person. This is especially difficult when the counselee's behavior is clearly prohibited by Scripture. The promiscuous man, for instance, probably doesn't need to be told that his sexual behavior is wrong. He knows this. But you can help him discover the sense of God's commands and perhaps lead him gently into obedience. Here the role of a Christian leader may differ from that of the psychologist. The pastor has an added spiritual responsibility and may see the need for rebuke or instruction.

Assign homework. Let the person do some work between sessions to continue the process. You may assign analytical projects: "Write down the story of what happened when you first felt this way." Or you may give therapeutic assignments: "Try smiling at people this week. Tell me what happens." Many people respond well to such projects, gaining a sense of accomplishment and progress. Avoid making assignments which cause too much anxiety, however.

Avoid fostering dependence, too. If you emerge as the problem solver for the troubled person, you may do little to build him or her up. The person may very well think, "I'm still no good, but my counselor makes me feel all right. He'll help me cope." If this becomes a problem, it would be wise to decrease the frequency of your sessions or refer the patient to another counselor.

Practical Assistance and Follow-up

Sometimes a single person needs help that's not psychological, but very practical. He or she needs a better job, a group of friends, a place to go for Christmas dinner. The major task of any counselor is to help the person cope with what is, but healing can be aided by a change of circumstance.

Single people are often among the neediest. Single parents may need child care, financial support, or a better-paying job. People who need to look for better work often need help getting started, compiling a resumé or contacting an employment agency.

Social contacts can be very helpful, especially for single people. Helpers should make good introductions whenever possible. This does not necessarily mean "fixing someone up" with a date; single people in crisis generally need friends of both sexes who can provide informal help and support.

When the counseling sessions are done, or you've referred the person to someone else, what happens? Unless you have managed to get your patient "married off" (which is not your job), he or she is still single. That's fine; singleness itself is not the problem.

But if the single person is still isolated, problems may recur. You may want to schedule a check-up meeting for six months later, or just keep an eye on the person for a while. It may be easy for him or her to fall back into old patterns.

Encourage the person to set up his or her own checkpoints—friends to be accountable to, regular lunches with the pastor or singles leader. And be sure the person knows you are available, even if only to find someone else who can help.

CHAPTER FOUR

CASE STUDIES

HOW DOES COUNSELING SINGLE PEOPLE WORK IN real life? The examples in this chapter, based on actual cases, will introduce you to the kinds of situations you may encounter—and how they might be handled.

Linda: She Couldn't Get Close

Linda was a 30-year-old schoolteacher, a Christian. Her roommate, Tracy, was 24 years old and socially active. While Tracy was out on dates and with friends, Linda would sit at home, feeling depressed. Lately, Linda had been having trouble getting along with Tracy, so she came to the counselor for help.

The counselor noticed that during the counseling sessions Linda would sit unusually far from him. So he asked her to keep talking, but to stand and face him and find the distance at which she felt most comfortable. She chose to stand nearly four feet away—over twice the distance most people choose for conversation. She also had trouble maintaining eye contact with the counselor.

As they talked, the counselor detected a pattern in Linda's history of relationships. All her life she had felt alienated from people. She could function at a distance from people, but had never had many friends. She would get close to a person—too close—and be rejected by him or her. That rejection would keep her from trusting people or getting close to them. Still, her need for friendship would soon lead her to establish another close relationship into which she would pour herself, usually pressuring the person or scaring him or her away. This led to more rejection, and the cycle would continue.

This pattern was being played out in the current conflict. Tracy was feeling pressured by Linda's dependence on her, so she was distancing herself from Linda. Linda reacted to this rejection with anger and depression.

The counselor concluded that Linda's root problem was her

feelings about herself. He made a series of "homework" assignments designed to help Linda feel more comfortable with people. He encouraged her to go to a grocery store and ask a clerk for help, or ask someone the time. In this way she might slowly learn to feel more at ease with social exchanges, and not be so dependent on Tracy.

The counselor also worked on reassuring Linda of her personal value. Tracing the pattern of her history helped her understand why she had been rejected so often, and made her feel better about herself.

Linda's progress was steady. The counselor cut the frequency of her visits from weekly to biweekly to monthly, and finally to "when you need me." The relationship between Linda and Tracy was restored, and they even began to double-date.

Emotional dependence on a friend or parent is a common problem among single people. One might expect single people to be independent, yet dependence keeps many from developing personally, from growing up, from "finding themselves."

Gary: One-Way Romance

Gary was a 38-year-old artist, a single man who was depressed. He came to the counselor complaining that he "couldn't do anything," artistically or otherwise.

Complicating the matter was his romantic interest in a woman ten years his junior. She was not interested in Gary to the same degree.

The counselor saw this as a case of emotional dependence. He tried to help Gary establish his independence, starting with his financial situation. The counselor helped Gary sell some of his paintings, thus beginning some spirals of success for him economically. That career success made Gary less likely to place so much importance on the relationship with the young woman.

Gary's case is an example of the practical assistance a counselor can sometimes give. This counselor was a painter himself, and thus was especially suited to help. Had the counselor lacked expertise in that area, perhaps he could have put Gary in touch with a church member who could help.

Gary's dependence on a romantic relationship is typical of many single people. They put off personal development while they pursue a relationship they hope will be fulfilling. Unfortunately, that very dependence can sometimes put too much pressure on those relationships, and they shatter. In any case, it is essential for a single person to learn to live singly in order to live happily.

Rachel: Trapped by a Parent

Rachel was a 25-year-old single woman who worked at a low-paying job as a receptionist in a law office. She lived at home with her neurotic, widowed mother. Rachel had a mild physical disability which kept her from competing aggressively in the social and economic world.

She came to the counselor, frustrated because she wanted independence but was not able to "wing it" financially. Even if she could have afforded to live on her own, she did not feel free to do so. Rachel felt the Bible's admonition to honor her mother meant living with her and attending to all her needs—though her mother was well able to provide for herself.

The counselor started by focusing on Rachel's financial problems. He discovered that Rachel had good skills that could be better used in another job. The counselor urged her to plan ahead, to plan for the way she might live as a single woman when she was 40 or 50.

At this writing, Rachel's case is in progress. The counselor plans to help Rachel see how she might compassionately yet firmly choose to move out and live on her own. If she chooses not to, the counselor could help her find ways to assert her independence within her current living situation. Presenting her with options would allow her a certain freedom, a certain independence, and would give her permission not to feel guilty.

Rachel's problem is fairly common among Christian single people, particularly women. The Biblical statement that "a man will leave his father and mother and be united to his wife" (Gen. 2:24) has some application to single people, too. Establishing one's independence from parents is necessary. Getting married provides a good opportunity to do so, but those who never marry need to make a similar break.

This isn't always easy, especially when parents don't want to let go. Since most people learn their basic sense of right and wrong from their parents, the sense of guilt over "cutting the apron strings" can be overwhelming and paralyzing. A counselor provides a new pair of eyes, and offers the single person permission to develop as an individual.

Fran: A Single Parent

Fran was a 34-year-old Christian woman with a three-year-old son—though she had never been married. She had a low-paying job as a housecleaner. She came to the counselor with a very specific crisis: Her son had been hurt, through her neglect, and a government agency had taken the child away.

Fran felt enormous guilt. Life seemed to be crushing down on her; she was helpless. She felt like a failure—unable to keep a man (her son's father), unable to get a good job, unable to care for her son. And she had no support from her family.

A bright spot here was her church, which offered Fran some financial assistance as well as social relationships. But still Fran saw no way out of her predicament.

The counselor first attempted to reassure her of God's providence and care for her. God had forgiven whatever sins she was feeling guilty for, and He had not forgotten about her. Next, the counselor helped her develop a plan for improving her lot—first economically, then doing whatever had to be done legally to get her son back.

Fran just couldn't handle things by herself. This is a common plight of single mothers. Unfortunately, they carry the stigma of sexual sin that keeps some Christians from responding lovingly. Even if Christians do respond with open arms, sometimes the single parent imagines disdain on their part. This may reflect his or her own guilt feelings. It takes strong efforts of support from involved Christians to overcome these barriers.

Beth: Hurt by Divorce

Beth was a 29-year-old single woman who taught second grade. She had been divorced a year earlier after several years of marriage, and had a two-year-old son in her custody. Her "presenting problem" when she came to the counselor was that she felt overly emotional all the time, with no rational reason for it. She wanted control over her emotions and "didn't want to get hurt."

The counselor could see that she was feeling rejected over the divorce, and perhaps guilty for her part in it. She was also angry about being left in the role of single parent. It was a difficult task to work and care for a two year old when her own support systems were gone.

In a sense, Beth was throwing a tantrum. Life was nothing like she wanted it to be. Her "happily ever after" ideals had been shattered. Had she been a child, she would have thrown herself on the floor and kicked her feet, screaming, "It's not fair!" But, as an adult, she had learned to force her emotions inside. That led to depression and inappropriate venting of the bottled-up emotions.

What a tantrum-throwing child wants more than anything else is attention. He or she wants to be picked up and cared for. Beth had a similar need.

The counselor met with Beth for several months. Together they achieved some success. The counselor provided the care, the listening ear, the sympathy Beth needed. She could go on from there to put her life back together.

Had the counselor not been there to help Beth with her anger, it might have festered for years, eating away at her personality. Some single people are like this—divorced or suffering from broken dating relationships, feeling they were wronged and refusing to let go of their grudges.

Forgiveness is the great righter of wrongs. Fran needed to accept the forgiveness God offers for whatever she may have done wrong. Beth needed to give it.

Some single people need to release the grudges they hold against God. They feel He has wronged them, failed them, not lived up to His promises. So they sulk, spiritually speaking. Sometimes this anger spills out as disobedience; sometimes it immobilizes the person.

Eric: Questioning God

Eric was a 29-year-old single man who taught learning-disabled children. He came to the counselor with questions about Christianity. Actually, though, he was struggling with the fact that he had found no one to marry.

Eric said he thought God wanted His children to be happy. So why hadn't He provided the one thing Eric needed to be happy—marriage?

The counselor needed to help Eric evaluate his expectations and compare them to God's promises. God hadn't promised a wife; He had promised a relationship with Himself.

The counselor tried to get Eric to face facts: "Since you may be single all your life, what will you do with your life?" This wasn't easy for Eric to accept. But as he talked with the counselor during their six sessions together, he began to see the logic of it. He decided to get on with his single life.

The counselor told us later, "This can be rough treatment, I know. Most people don't want to face such a question, but it is important for single people to establish lives of their own, apart from marriage—rather than setting all their hopes for personal advancement on some future marriage which may or may not occur.

"If people really press the issue, I'll say, 'Fine. If your goal is to be married, how will you go about making that happen?' "

Nate: Sexual Confusion

Singleness can prompt some to question their own sexuality. Some who have never been strongly attracted to the opposite sex may begin to wonder whether they are homosexual. Even their wondering may make them feel guilty: Are they sinning by merely thinking about it? Others experiment.

Nate was a 23-year-old single man, a graduate student at a major university. He came to the counselor with a sense of anxiety. He was concerned about the fantasies he was having, particularly homosexual fantasies. Though he had had no overt homosexual experiences, he feared that his thoughts might indicate a tendency in that direction.

The counselor discovered in Nate's history a pattern of rejection. Love had always brought pain. Nate was an adopted child, and in his relationships love had always ultimately led to his being rejected. His homosexual fantasies stemmed from his fear of relationships. Expressing himself sexually would be safest with men, or so his subconscious mind deduced.

Nate had recently become a Christian and was sorting through the requirements of his faith. This may have added to his anxiety.

When the counselor unearthed this history of rejection, it was an exciting burst of insight for Nate, a freeing experience. It explained his fantasies and convinced him that this was not necessarily some innate predisposition he could never conquer.

Mary: The Grieving Widow

Many single people are widowed or divorced. These circumstances cause problems all their own, but the widowed and divorced, like the never married, must often deal with their problems alone. This can result in unresolved anger, unrealistic self-expectations, and emotional paralysis.

Mary was a 58-year-old widow who worked as a medical technician. She had three children in their 20s who were doing well. Her husband, a writer, had just died suddenly. This had upended Mary's world.

Mary felt that, as a Christian, she should not grieve. God's will had been done, she reasoned; she would see her husband in Heaven. Christians should be happy, she thought. One day of grieving should be sufficient; no need to carry on one's bereavement. Mary felt guilty for feeling sad, though she wouldn't let it show.

The counselor observed in Mary a great deal of underlying anger, which she was suppressing. During his three sessions with her, the counselor assured her that six months to a year of grief is normal. It was proper for her to feel sorrow and rejection and even anger, since this had been such a major upheaval. She needed to let her family and friends and church care for her during this time.

Six months later, Mary showed up again at the counselor's office. She had gone through the grieving process and was ready to reconstruct her life.

Now the counselor needed to attend to practical needs. Mary had not worked for several years, so the counselor helped her prepare a resumé and encouraged her to go job hunting. She managed to get a job in her field. The counselor further encouraged her to go out and do fun things with friends, to go to the hairdresser and take pride in her appearance again, and to invite people over—all of which she did. After five sessions, she didn't need to return.

Here again we see the counselor offering permission. Like so many single people, Mary needed to be told that it was okay to feel her emotions—and then to get on with the single life.

CHAPTER FIVE

QUESTIONS AND ANSWERS

WHAT CAN YOU SAY TO THE HURTING, QUESTIONING SINgle person? This chapter contains questions single people often ask—or would ask if they found a listening ear. Feel free to adapt the suggested answers to your own situation and that of the questioner.

Why do I keep hearing about "the gift of singleness"? I'm single, but as far as I'm concerned it's no "gift."

There are two kinds of gifts. One is like a birthday present, which you receive with gratitude and perhaps use for a while. The other is like a talent, which you can discover and develop and use for the glory of God.

If you are single, that is God's "present" to you—at least for now. You may not want it. You may wish the package you unwrapped had contained a marriage. You may want to take it back to the "store" and exchange it for something else. That's understandable.

But let's try to understand that feeling a little better. Say it's your ninth birthday. You want a bicycle; your mom gives you new clothes. Of course you're disappointed—but you need to realize two things:

1. Mom loves you, and her gift of new clothes is an expression of her love. It is the thought that counts. More important, it is the *relationship* that counts.

2. Mother knows best. When you are that age, she knows better than you do what you need. She may worry that you aren't ready for the bike you want; you might get hurt riding it. Next year, though, you may get a three-speed.

Those are the two things to remember about God's gift of singleness. It is an expression of His love for you, and He knows best what you need.

But what about that other kind of gift? If you see other people who seem talented at being single, and you aren't, join the club.

Few are so gifted. Some who seem that way are faking it; others have arrived there only after years of struggle.

It's a matter of acceptance. Ada Lum, veteran single missionary for InterVarsity Christian Fellowship, says you have three choices: to live in perpetual frustration; to resign yourself to "subhuman" existence, which dishonors God; or to accept your state joyfully, because it is from God.

As long as you're going to be single, you might as well get good at it. Learn the advantages of singleness and use them. Prepare for the down times; enjoy the good times. Like any other talent, a propensity for singleness needs to be developed, practiced. You won't be an instant success.

The "gift of singleness" is not just some pious euphemism. Think of it as a tennis racket you get for Christmas: you receive it, accept it (acknowledging your relationship to the giver), and then use it, determining to practice every day until you're the best tennis player you can be.

I keep analyzing myself to find what my problem is—the defect that keeps me single. Am I unmarried because there's something about me that has to change?

Maybe, but probably not. If you're thinking of marriage as some great prize which you haven't yet qualified for, forget it. Just because you're single does not mean there is something wrong with you.

All of us, married or not, have things about us that should change. It's possible that there are features of your personality that are preventing you from getting involved with others. If you can't identify those traits, we could look for them together and work on them. But you won't reach perfection. And you may not find a mate (though you'll probably gain more good friends).

Marriage is not a reward for being a better person. Self-improvement is its own reward. The most attractive thing about a person is his or her Christlike character. If you develop this, with God's help, you'll grow closer to Christ, bring glory to His name, build up His Body—and then you will have gained immeasurably, whether or not you end up married.

All my life I've been taught that getting married is what people do when they grow up. I'm 32, but single. I feel stuck somewhere in time, unable to become an adult. What can I do?

The majority of the population does get married. But those who don't are less in number—not less in value or maturity.

The feeling of not fitting into adulthood is common for single people and married people. There are plenty of parents who feel as if they're still in college, and older folks who are surprised when they hit 55. Surround yourself with a wide range of people in all sorts of stages of life. Accept them for who they are and not on the basis of their age or marital status, and they will probably begin to accept you on the same terms.

I'm beginning to think I will never get married. But I hate the thought of becoming an "old maid." How can I deal with this?

Walter Trobisch's comments may help:

> What is an "old maid"? Someone unable to love. Someone who represses her feelings and doesn't say yes to herself. There are teenage old maids. There are also married old maids. There are even male old maids.
>
> The opposite of the old maid is the virgin. Virginity is not something negative, but something tremendously positive. It corresponds to the demands of our deepest nature. Virginity is preparedness for the fullness of love.[1]

Trobisch is not just playing semantic games here. He is saying something important about the way men and women look at themselves.

Why are you so afraid of being an "old maid"—or, if you were male, of going through life as a bachelor? It's the image you resent. You don't like that image of yourself as someone the world has passed by, unloved, unloving. But you don't have to think that way. You don't have to wait for anybody else to accept you.

Accept yourself, whatever your marital state. Free yourself to show love to others as you allow yourself to be loved by others. In this way, you determine the kind of person you become, with the guidance and strength of the Lord. You are not at the mercy of the labels and whims of others.

All my sisters and brothers are married with children. When I go home my mother never fails to ask if I've found a girlfriend, and looks hurt when I say no. It makes me feel like a failure to have no prospects for marriage. How can I handle this?

Family pressures are among the strongest we feel in any

matter. We grow up looking to our parents for approval and we never completely outgrow that. That feeling of failure will be hard to shake.

But you are grown up now, and making decisions for yourself. Your mother means well, and in many cases her advice is valuable. But here the pressure she puts on you is less than helpful.

Talk to her about it. She probably doesn't realize how you react to her simple questions. Remember, your reactions are very normal. Ask her to help you out by easing up on the pressure.

Talk with her about what it would be like if you never married. That would be okay, wouldn't it? And if you did marry, would that solve all your problems? Of course not. Assure her (and yourself) that your best course of action is to learn to live successfully on your own. Then, if a marriage happens, great! If not, fine. Your success or failure in life does not ride on whether or not you marry.

Of course, talking may not change anything. Your mother, and the rest of your family, may continue to pressure you in various ways. You need to turn off that pressure, to put it in its place. You need to convince yourself of your own personal value as a single person. Those who pressure you to marry may mean well, but they are misguided in this case.

My church singles group is like a meat market. At least that's how I feel when I'm there. How should I deal with this?

In their book, Singles: The New Americans (New American Library, 1983) Jacqueline Simenauer and David Carroll discovered a fascinating phenomenon. Interviewing people who patronized singles bars, they found that most complained about how dehumanizing the bars were—yet they showed up night after night! The point is that these people were both the victims and the causes of that dehumanization.

You feel as if your singles group is a meat market, dehumanizing. That may be because you are dehumanizing yourself and others. How? Through snap judgments, narrow expectations, and poor self-image.

Snap judgments: According to some researchers, the average conversation in a singles bar lasts seven seconds. That doesn't include the half hour of eyeing each other across the room, or (nowadays) the ten or fifteen seconds of checking out each other's medical history. But the fact is that most singles bar decisions are based on nothing deeper than appearance.

Church singles groups should be different. Most are. But *you* need to make that difference. As you take the time to get to know someone else on a deeper level, he or she will be getting to know you. You'll feel less like a slab of beef.

Narrow expectations: Why do you go to singles group activities? To find a spouse? To prove to the assembled members of the opposite sex that you would make a great husband or wife? These may be valid reasons, but they are just two among many. If you meet each man as a potential husband, each woman as a potential wife, and you listen for wedding bells, no wonder it seems like a meat market.

Expand your perspective. Find *friends* in your singles group. Forget the wedding bells; they'll just keep you from hearing what your friends are really saying.

Poor self-image: Are you afraid you won't measure up to the standards of others in your singles group? Maybe that's why you feel disapproving gazes on you as you walk across the room. Maybe that's why you imagine them holding up rating cards as you pass—five-point-five, six-point-two. Maybe they are ready to accept you, but you are judging yourself.

Sure, there will always be some who play the judging game. But most of the people in your singles group are probably just as unhappy with the "meat market" as you are. If you accept them, they'll accept you.

Why doesn't our church have a singles ministry? Why should I stay here if the church doesn't care about singles?

Your church may have decided it didn't need a singles ministry because single people fit so well into the other ministries of the church. That is, it views single people as *real* people and sees no need to shunt them off into a separate group. If this is the case, enjoy it.

It is also possible that your church would like to have a singles group but lacks the leadership. A singles group usually needs at least one strong leader and a core group of four or five. Could you, perhaps, provide the leadership for such a group, or pull together some core members?

Maybe your church doesn't have enough single people to form a special group. Or perhaps the leaders of your church have never really thought about it. If so, you need to talk with the pastor or board and voice your concerns.

Why should you stay? First, because you can't assume the church doesn't care about singles in general or you in particular. Second, because the church does not exist merely to meet your needs. The Lord may lead you to find another church, but don't make that decision hastily.

If you find you need a singles group, consider getting involved with another church's singles activities while remaining active in your own church. Communicate with people in both churches about what you are doing.

The whole dating system is crazy. I'll never find a mate this way. What am I supposed to do?

The world defines dating in terms of physical beauty, material wealth, competition, score keeping. Such self-centered practices are wrong. But Christian dating doesn't have to be like that.

Christians should be able to look more deeply at others, beyond physical appearance. Christians should be able to avoid the sexual pressure of secular dating and get to know each other in fuller ways. Christians should be less selfish and more sensitive as they date.

Alas, it doesn't always work this way. We adopt secular models for our dating routines and find ourselves playing the same games as the world does. These games result in crises of varying proportions:

1. *No one wants to go out with me.* For some the solution is simple: Stop waiting for others to ask you and start asking them. Some Christian women feel it inappropriate to ask a man to go out. They can find more subtle ways to indicate their interest. The key is to take action rather than waiting for things to happen.

But for many the problem is much more acute. These are the people who, because of physical appearance, disability, or lack of social skills, find themselves "unmarketable." It's sad that we have to talk of marketing in relation to people, but this is the world's dating system, which Christians too often follow. It is important for such people to see the "dating market" for what it is—silly, arbitrary, dehumanizing even for its winners. They need to see their own value as people apart from that system.

It may help to get involved in group activities as much as possible. That gives one a chance to know and be known in a casual setting. Perhaps the broader interaction might lead to later one-to-one relationships.

2. *I want to date casually, but the other person is getting serious.* Some dating relationships can survive (but not thrive) for a long time without basic communication. Single people get together and do things, but can easily forget to talk. Assumptions can be made which need to be checked at regular intervals.

Long-term relationships go through a certain focusing as they progress. At first, both people may be dating others as well; then they focus on each other and spend more and more time together. Crises can occur when one person feels further along in the process than the other does. Sometimes the desire to avoid pain keeps those involved from communicating, but they must talk it out.

3. *I want to get romantic, but to him I'm just a "sister in Christ."* This is a common frustration among Christians.

What to do? Don't disparage what you have. A deep brother-sister friendship is often more fulfilling than a romance with that person would be.

Communicate your desires, but don't force the issue. Try not to jeopardize the friendship you have.

Reexamine your idea of romance. Is it really love you're looking for, or some fantasy image?

Allow this friendship to build you up rather than tear you down. That is, when you're with this friend, keep thinking, "I'm glad this person thinks enough of me to be my friend," rather than, "I'm sorry this person doesn't think enough of me to be my lover."

4. *I've been dating a non-Christian and it is getting serious.* While it is right for Christians to be friends with non-Christians, it is wrong to marry an unbeliever (II Cor. 6:14). Dating is somewhere in between. Many Christians, entering such relationships casually, soon find them growing too serious. Some are so "in love" that they make all sorts of rationalizations. Some fear that they will never find a Christian mate as good as this non-Christian one. Most of them hope and pray that they will lead their partners to the Lord, but this seldom happens. Often the partners lead the Christians away from the Lord.

Both parties should get the ground rules straight, agreeing that there will be no marriage unless both are Christians. It is extremely difficult to cut back on a serious relationship, but it's either that or a total breakup.

There will be pain. There may be anger at God for not making the other person a Christian. There is danger of spiritual shipwreck, so the loving support of the Christian community is crucial.

5. *There are no Christians worth dating.* This statement smacks of the surface judgment of the secular dating system. "All the Christian women I know are dogs." "All the Christian men are nerds." Christians must learn to see beyond the surface. There are some wonderful people hiding behind so-so looks and imperfect social skills.

Reexamine your assumptions. Are there Christian traits that you find inherently "nerdy" or homely? Are there un-Christian traits you find attractive? It is not easy to overhaul your value system, but it is an important way to survive as a Christian in a mixed-up dating scene.

I'm so lonely I physically ache. I try not to feel sorry for myself, but what can I do? I can't stand the thought of attending some of the church "socials," and I certainly can't go to a bar.

Loneliness can be a gnawing, debilitating frame of mind. It feeds on itself, sometimes keeping you from doing things that would alleviate your loneliness. The solution—a difficult one—is to break that spiral.

There are two approaches. First, you can learn to live with your loneliness. Second, you can attack some of its causes.

The first way of living with loneliness is to learn to like yourself. The second is to know God better. Take advantage of your time alone to get closer to the Lord. This is not to say that a richer devotional life will cure your loneliness, but it is a way of dealing with it. It should make your lonely feelings less debilitating and free you to take some therapeutic steps.

Now you need to get at the causes of your loneliness. Are you like many lonely people who work in crowded offices or factories, but feel no one knows them? An unfulfilled desire to be known fuels their loneliness. Yet a fear of being known keeps many of them from deeper relationships. They are afraid people will reject them once they are really known.

You say you "can't stand the thought of attending some of the church socials." Why? Are you afraid that the superficial nature of the conversations there will just tease you and make you feel more "unknown" than ever? Or are you afraid that you will be forced to divulge more of who you are, and risk the judgment of others?

Here's where that time alone can support you. Your Bible study should be telling you that you are important to God, made in His image. You have plenty to offer others. Your self-liking should be making you more comfortable, more confident, more able to take risks.

So go to that social; take a chance. Call a friend just to chat on the phone. Invite a friend out for pizza. Volunteer to work as a tutor or a helper in some service organization. Let yourself be known by others. Even if you are rejected, you can rest secure in God's acceptance and your own acceptance of yourself.

This will not erase loneliness from your life. There will always be lonely times. But it can break that spiral, and help you cope when times are difficult.

I hate coming home to an empty apartment. At the end of the workday, I get this very sad feeling. Sometimes it makes me go out at night to bars, just because I can't stand staying home. What can I do?

You could get a roommate. That might make home a little less lonely. How about changing your surroundings? Put some pictures on the walls, make it a fun place to be. As Janice Harayda writes, "Happy single people tend to live with their homes, not just in them."[2] Get into the habit of inviting people over on a regular basis. Start a weekly Bible study or rent a video each week and invite friends over.

My boyfriend said good-bye last week. This is the fourth serious relationship in three years. At this rate I'll never get married. I am angry and defensive and scared of ever trying again. Is there something wrong with me?

Your feelings are natural and understandable. Failed relationships can cause major crises for single people. They can be similar to divorce, though not generally as severe. There is usually a grieving process involved, and strong feelings of self-doubt.

Is something wrong with you? If so, it's probably something you can change. Maybe you are pushing too hard, too fast, in these relationships. Maybe you are always rebounding from one serious relationship to another without pausing to evaluate what's happened. The fact that you have had four "serious" relationships in three years may indicate that you are rushing things.

Are you grounding your identity in some hoped-for marriage, rather than feeling complete and secure in yourself as God's child? Some women search endlessly for a man to bring meaning to their lives; some men seek fulfillment in relationships with women. This approach leads most to disappointment and comes dangerously close to idolatry.

It's natural for you to want comfort in this time of "bereavement" over your latest relationship. It's natural for you to seek signs that you are still attractive to men. But it's probably best not to seek this comfort in another romantic relationship—at least not yet. Rely on Christian friends for the support you need and, most of all, put your trust in God.

I'm a single woman with a good friendship with a married couple. I find myself growing more and more attracted to the husband. I've even started dreaming about him. What should I do?

Don't think that you're immune to sin in this relationship. The least that might happen is the warping of a good friendship due to your infatuation. The worst is a marriage destroyed by adultery. Take the situation seriously.

You need to decide at least three things: how much to draw back from the relationship, whether or not to let the reason be known, and why you find yourself infatuated. Your course of action may depend on which is stronger, your friendship with the couple or your attraction.

Examine the reasons for your feelings. Confide in a friend or counselor who will hold you accountable for your actions. If your attraction is still too strong to handle a friendship with the couple, you will have to withdraw somewhat. This may be temporary, until you can tame your feelings. It may not be necessary or helpful to share your feelings with the couple; it might even be damaging.

I recently went through a painful divorce. As a result I find myself shying away from contact with anyone of the opposite sex. This is keeping me from developing friendships and beginning to affect my everyday life. What should I do?

As with bereavement, there is a necessary grieving process during and after a divorce. So allow yourself some time to adjust.

Keep reminding yourself of the basic facts. Your spouse was one member of the opposite sex, hardly representative of the whole gender. There are still some wonderful people out there with whom you can form friendships. Try to accept them on their own terms.

For now, try developing some friendships with people of your own sex. These friends should help you adjust.

My husband left me a few years ago. At first my married friends were very supportive. But since the divorce was finalized, they seem to shut me out more and more. It's as if I'm diseased or something. I long to have these friendships back, but what can I do?

It's confusing, isn't it? You are the same person, but your category has changed, and that affects how people treat you. It generally happens quite innocently. Couples do things with other couples, so when they're planning things, now they overlook you. They don't mean to; they just do.

There is also a subconscious "disease" mentality. Deep down, most couples are afraid of divorce. They fear it might happen to them. You, by your presence, are a reminder that divorce does happen and that it hurts. They'd rather not think about that, so they tend to exclude you.

Can you talk with your friends about your feelings? Ask for their support. Don't scold them for their insensitivity. In most cases, it's unintentional. You should be able to improve things just by bringing it to their attention.

Another course of action is to find some new friends. If you always find yourself squeezed out of the company of your married friends, look for lonely people and reach out to them in friendship. These new relationships may prove just as supportive as the old ones.

I was widowed about a year ago. It has been a lonely time, and I'm still adjusting. Now my friends are telling me I should get out and socialize, look for a new mate. But I don't know whether I can make it in the singles world. Do I have to?

Take your time. Don't worry about whether you "should"

date. Each person has his or her own timetable for adjusting to widowhood.

Try reminding yourself of a few things. First, remarriage is not necessarily the answer. A hasty move to marry may cause more problems than it solves. Second, a solid support network of friends can help meet many of your needs. Don't be afraid to ask your friends for help—emotional support, companionship, or practical assistance in tending a home by yourself. Third, you don't have to play "dating games." Don't let that "singles world" terrify you so. Try to relax and be yourself. Church and friends can help you make new acquaintances.

I can't believe sex is always wrong outside marriage. Why would God make us so miserable?

Most cultures in human history have agreed that marriage is sacrosanct, and that sex is a part of marriage. Even so, Christians can't take any culture's mores as the standard. We must start at the point of accepting the Bible as God's authoritative Word for our lives.

Throughout the Old and New Testaments marriage is held to be sacred. Sexual relations are treated as holy. The Bible clearly condemns fornication and adultery—that is, sexual relations outside marriage. What belongs within marriage becomes wrong outside it.

Those are the rules. If you believe the Bible, you must agree that God wants sex reserved for marriage.

Why? We may never know fully. Perhaps it has to do with creation. Sexual intercourse is a holy act because it is the act by which babies are made. In a sense, we mirror God's creative activity when we create human life—and thus the actions associated with procreation are held sacred. God wants procreation to happen within love, within family, within marriage. That is the context for this holy act.

In ancient Israel, there was a day on which the high priest could perform sacrifice in the Holiest Place of the tabernacle. Within the context of the Day of Atonement, it was a wonderful, holy action. On any other day it would have been terribly wrong. In the same way, sexual relations within marriage are lovely, holy acts, but outside that context they are sacrilege.

Does that make single people miserable? It shouldn't have to. Perhaps what makes us miserable is the doctrine our culture keeps preaching at us—that sex is everything. Everywhere we turn we're told in one form or another that intercourse is the highest pleasure life has to offer, that chastity is psychologically damaging, that sexual fulfillment is necessary for human wholeness. With that sort of pressure it's easy to focus on what you can't have—sexual intercourse—and blow it out of proportion.

God calls His unmarried children to chastity. He does not "doom" them to a lack of pleasure or passion; there are other sources of pleasure and passion.

Does that make you a "neuter," neither male nor female, just single and chaste? Can you be a "real" man or woman without "having sex"? The fact is that we all "have" sex—that is, we possess sexuality, we are male and female. Our sexuality exists independently of our behavior. Jesus was a sexual being, though He did not marry. To be human is to be sexual.

To express our humanity is to express our sexuality. To be involved with people, to feel a range of emotions, to work and be creative, to play and rest and think—all these human activities involve our being, our sexuality.

So what am I supposed to do with my sex drive? How do I live with unfulfilled desires?

First, know the Biblical limits of sexual behavior and the reasons behind them—and know your own body and what to expect from it. Remember, your sex drive is not the bulldozer everybody says it is. It can be tamed. It seems so strong because the world tells you again and again that you can't fight it. When you get the right perspective on things, the pressure should ease.

Second, know the forces and circumstances that give you the most trouble—and avoid them! Alcoholics know that if they walk into a bar, they walk into trouble. If you fill your mind with sexual images and fantasies, you doom yourself to sin, misery, or both.

Third, know that God—who created sex, designed your body, and commanded you to live purely—will give you the grace to obey Him joyfully.

My sexually active past makes abstinence unbearable. I'm having an awful time with fantasies and memories.

Here is a Biblical truth to start with: There is no temptation stronger than God's power to help you overcome it. You might memorize I Corinthians 10:13.

When do you have these fantasies and memories? What starts them? Try to break the chain of thoughts that leads to them. Decide on an action you'll take as soon as you start to fantasize, such as saying out loud, "Stop it!" (if you live alone) or doing 20 jumping jacks. This may sound melodramatic, but it works. Choose a topic to start thinking about to replace the unrighteous pictures that crop up in your mind—something completely different, and lighter, like the fate of the Mets or a favorite comic book character.

If you fail, ask for God's forgiveness and strength—and keep making progress a step at a time.

My girlfriend and I want to please the Lord. But we are getting more and more physically involved, though we stop short of intercourse. Is there anything wrong with "petting"?

In other words, how far can you go without sinning? There are differing opinions among Christian leaders. One expert says that the key question is to ask yourself, "At what point does the body begin to prepare itself for intercourse?"[3] Since intercourse is forbidden outside marriage, it makes sense that foreplay is also wrong.

In general, premarital sexual fondling reaps more trouble than it's worth. It's frustrating; it naturally escalates itself, and draws the two people into a relationship more serious than they're ready for. It makes exploring one another's character and spiritual nature much less appealing by comparison. It can also lead to unpremeditated, but real, sin.

You obviously feel you have gone too far. Stop your physical involvement. Talk about it. Set limits. It is never easy to go backward in physical intimacy, but it is often essential if you want to get your relationship back in balance. It takes regular communication and double discipline. Don't rely on the other person to say no. Both must draw the line and accept responsibility for staying within its bounds.

Some counselors recommend abstaining from all physical contact, even simple kissing, for a set period of time. Use this time to get to know each other spiritually, emotionally, and intellectually. Even though kissing may not be wrong, a time of such abstinence could help get the physical aspects of a relationship in balance with the rest.

If you are engaged, consider advancing the wedding date. Unnecessarily long engagements can put needless pressure on a couple.

I've sinned by having sex with my boyfriend. Does this mean that, in God's eyes, we're married to each other? Should I go ahead and marry him now, since I have lost my virginity to him?

You have recognized that having intercourse outside of marriage is a sin, and presumably you have repented. But marriage will not make that sin holy; only the blood of Jesus Christ can remove sin. That blood has already bought your forgiveness.

Don't make things worse by rushing into marriage. Accept God's forgiveness and start anew. Time, prayer, other Christians' advice, getting to know each other nonsexually, and submitting together to God's will should show you and your boyfriend whether marriage is for you.

I'm still a virgin. Why wait for a husband if one is never going to arrive?

You have probably guarded your virginity through the years because you wanted to save it for your husband. That is a lovely thought, to give your virginity as a present to your husband, and it's an idea that God loves. But it is not the best reason to remain a virgin.

More than anything else, you should say no to sexual relations in order to please God. God has clearly forbidden premarital sex. He is the main One to whom your virginity is a gift. If you marry, you will please your husband, too, but your husband will be the second recipient of your purity. Not having a husband "to save yourself for" makes no difference. You still have God to please.

I feel guilty about masturbating and want to stop, but can't. That makes me feel worse. What can I do?

There are two basic approaches to this problem. One says, "There's nothing wrong with masturbation, so why feel guilty?" The other says, "It is wrong, and you must stop." Either way, the problem is real, and very common.

Because masturbation involves our sexuality, it involves the deepest part of ourselves and our relationship to our Creator. It must not be dismissed carelessly one way or another.

Christians are divided concerning the morality of masturbation. Some say that because it is sexual activity outside marriage, it is wrong—period. Others believe it is a legitimate method for the unmarried to relieve sexual tension. Still others think it can be both, though it is not the ideal and must be decided upon by each individual.

It is not a sickness, nor does it stunt growth or cause impotence. The Bible says nothing explicit about masturbation, though various passages (Gen. 38:8-10; Mic. 2:1) have been misinterpreted as prohibitions against it. Most experts consider it typical of adolescent development, especially among boys. So what is it about masturbation that causes such controversy?

First, sexuality involves communication. The sex act, meant only for marriage, bonds two people into "one flesh"; the husband and wife are thus known more intimately by each other than by any other person. What sort of communication does masturbation accomplish? None. Walter and Ingrid Trobisch, in their book *My Beautiful Feeling*, say this: "It divides a person in two, for he must play two incompatible roles simultaneously—that of the stimulus giver and stimulus receiver. . . . No communication, no relationship emerges from it. The person speaks to no one and gives to no one; he only takes something from himself." [4]

Second, masturbation involves a person's thoughts. Some claim that masturbation aids in self-control, yet often the result is the reverse. Lust leads to more lust. Masturbation may not be expressly prohibited by the Word of God, but lust is.

This is clear: If practiced compulsively, or in a way that involves lust, or with the aid of pornographic images, then masturbation is not for the Christian. Beyond that, you must prayerfully decide whether or not masturbation is sin for you.

Your guilt has made that decision for you. You find yourself enslaved by this habit, and being a slave to one's desires is wrong. Whether or not occasional masturbation is permissible is not the issue with you. For you it is a compulsion, and a damaging one.

Tell God you're sorry and accept His forgiveness. Ask for His help in overcoming this problem. Then think about what your life would be like without masturbation. That *is* possible. One of the biggest problems you face is the feeling that you "can't" win. Imagine yourself overcoming this, and trust God that He will help you make it happen.

Analyze your life-style. When do you masturbate? At regular times each day? What prompts you to do so? Identify the problem areas and change them. Establish alternative habits for the times you usually masturbate. Go jogging. Study Scripture. Write letters.

Avoid unhealthy thoughts and images. Say no to all forms of pornography. Be careful about the TV shows and movies you watch, the music you listen to. Turn things off when they start tempting you. Walk away.

Establish accountability if you can. Confide in a close friend, pastor, or counselor who will check up on you. Be honest with that person.

Finally, recognize that there may be other emotional needs sparking this habit. The Trobisches say that habitual masturbation is often a symptom of something nonsexual, such as dissatisfaction with one's self or anger toward God. Try to figure out the why of your action, and work at that level for a solution.

My relatives are beginning to wonder whether I'm gay, since I'm not married. The fact is, I am much more comfortable around those of my own sex. Am I a homosexual without realizing it?

It is perfectly normal at certain times in one's development to feel more affinity with one's own sex and uncomfortable with the opposite sex. Perhaps something in your upbringing has stalled you at a certain stage of development or thrown you back to it. If you have never learned how to interact with the opposite sex, the prospect can be a frightening one.

What should you do about it? First of all, reject the notion that you must be a homosexual. If homosexual temptations arise, say no to them. Don't indulge fantasies of that kind.

Make an effort to establish relationships with people of the opposite sex. Don't expect it to be easy or even comfortable at first, but as you develop friendships the barriers should fall. Avoid comparing yourself with others who are further along in this process than you are.

It may be that you will never feel "attracted" to the opposite sex. Don't assume that this means you must be attracted to those of your own gender. It may be that God is giving you a special gift for singleness and relieving you of the distractions that romance might offer.

As for your relatives, don't worry too much about their suspicions. The best you can do is to show them how much you love the Lord. Through kindness and joy and righteousness, prove yourself to them as a sincere follower of Christ, and let them draw whatever conclusions they wish.

I've prayed for a husband, and no man has shown up. Who says God answers prayer?

Your question reveals a great deal of pain and disappointment. This is something you want very much, and God has denied you this pleasure, seemingly for no good reason.

The Bible does talk about God answering prayers and granting requests. But, when we look at the whole pattern of Scripture, some important qualifications emerge. They might be summed up under Jesus' phrase: "Thy will be done." As our desires conform to God's desires, we find ourselves, in essence, wanting what God gives us.

We are to pray "in Jesus' name." That's more than a saying to tack onto our prayers. It means that we seek Jesus' glory above all else. Thus an ideal prayer might be something like, "Lord, I believe I could glorify You most by being married, so please send me a husband. But if You would rather have me glorify You as a single woman, Your will be done."

So, why pray? If God is going to do His will anyway, what's the use?

Prayer keeps you in touch with God. Each time you make your requests, you acknowledge God as the Giver of all good things. As you "listen" in prayer, you may find your own wants becoming more like God's. Finally, although we may not always know where to fit this in our theology, the Bible does indicate that occasionally God changes His mind in response to the prayers of His people.

God does care about you very much. Keep praying. As you pray, trust and listen. Trust that God wants to do whatever is best for you. And listen for His ideas of what that best is all about.

I'm a 38-year-old single woman. It's extremely unlikely that I'll ever have a child. How can I deal with that?

Let's explore the way you feel about this. Are you mad at God? Do you feel half-human? Do you secretly think God must have judged you unworthy of mothering children?

The Biblical purpose of women isn't to bear and nurture children. It's to glorify and please God. Some do this through motherhood, but there are many other means. In fact, Scripture indicates that your lack of family responsibility better enables you to serve God in other ways. God may have chosen not to lead you into marriage and child rearing because He has even better things in mind for you.

But you still want children, right? And it makes you angry at God that He hasn't given motherhood to you. Tell Him so! Be honest. Tell Him what you want. Ask Him what He wants. Don't harbor your anger; let Him have it. It's no miracle cure, but at least you and God will still be talking. Somewhere in that process you may find that God loves you and knows what's best for you.

It might also be helpful to find a group of women with whom you can be honest and share your pain and disappointment. Ask for their prayer and listen to their counsel. Look for other ways to use your God-given desire to nurture, like becoming an "aunt" or a godparent to your friends' children, or working in the church nursery or Sunday School. Perhaps you could tutor an underprivileged child or disciple a teenager. You may focus less on what you don't have when you give others what you do have.

What's the use of being a Christian? I have tried to honor God, withstanding temptation throughout my single life, and God has not honored that. Here I am, 35, and still not married. Why hasn't God been good to me when I've been so good to Him?

Can you earn favors from God? Does He work that way? The Bible seems to indicate that God gives His grace freely and works out the matters of our lives in the ways that are best for us.

Righteousness is its own reward. If you had given in to temptation along the way, your life might be a mess right now, because sin destroys. If you stop declaring that God owes you and start thanking Him for what He has given, you will be a lot happier.

Once you deal with those feelings, you can do two constructive things. First, plan to be single. If you knew you were going to be single for the rest of your life, what would you do? How would you live? Stop waiting to get married and start building your own life.

Second, if you really want to get married, how will you go

about doing that? Take some initiative, with God's guidance. Don't wait for Him to bring someone to your doorstep. Make a move.

Now you win either way. You either get married, or you are free to live the contented single life you'll be building.

A Theology of Singleness

Many single people have problems that stem, at least in part, from the way they view the world, themselves, and God. That is, they have bad theology.

They may be angry at God because they expect certain things that He doesn't deliver. They may struggle with feelings of inferiority because they have wrong ideas about creation. They may be overwhelmed by sexual temptation because they lack a Biblical sexual ethic.

Not all emotional or psychological problems are, at root, spiritual or theological. Nor is preaching at single people in crisis the best way to help them. But Christian ministry to hurting single people should be grounded on a Biblical theology of singleness. As counselors and counselees develop sound ideas about God and humanity, they lay a solid foundation for healing.

With that in mind, this chapter looks at several aspects of "single" theology: the value of single people; single people and the image of God; the advantages of marriage and singleness; being called to a single life; and the sexuality of single people.

Is Singleness Okay?

When God created the heavens and the earth, after each day He took stock of what He had done and declared it good. Finally He made Adam and took Eve out of the man's side. Did God look at what He had made and say, "There goes the neighborhood—it was nice here until you folks showed up"? No! He called the first people "very good." Humanity had capped God's Creation.

That is where a theology of singleness begins—with God making human beings in His image and declaring them good. Note that God made an individual human being first. Later he made humanity a couple. We can infer that each person, married or single, is made in God's image—the pinnacle of God's "very good" Creation.

But wait. Something in the Creation story is declared *not* good. ''The Lord God said, 'It is not good for the man to be alone. I will make a helper suitable for him' '' (Gen. 2:18). Then God made woman.

God did not find Adam's aloneness desirable. The reader might gather from this that only married people are part of God's ''very good'' creation, and that single people, being alone, are ''not good.''

But why was it bad for Adam to be alone? Many have assumed that he needed a wife, but that is not exactly what the text says. Most commentators indicate that man was made as a social being and thus needed another human as a companion. The fact that God made man ''male and female'' means not necessarily that man was made to marry, but that God intended for human beings to relate to other human beings.

Notice also what God did to change Adam's aloneness. He gave Adam a ''suitable helper.'' Why did God use those terms? Why didn't He give the man a ''close friend,'' an ''intimate companion,'' or even a ''loving wife''?

Eve certainly must have been all of the above, but the Biblical emphasis is mainly on work, not fellowship. What Adam needed was not so much a companion, but a ''helper.'' He had been given a colossal task to do, tending the garden (2:15) and naming the animals (2:19-20). He needed help!

With woman as a ''suitable helper,'' there would be two workers in the Garden—not to mention the children they would have. In fact, God makes this desire for more workers explicit in Genesis 1:28—''Be fruitful and increase in number; fill the earth and subdue it.''

So what was God declaring ''not good''? It was the possibility that there would always be only one man in the Garden, overworked, with no one to help. If God was to have an earth full of human beings worshiping Him and caring for His creation, He needed woman as a helper to co-tend the Garden and help build the human race.

Does that mean single people are disobeying God by not marrying and having children? We might assume this, except that the New Testament says otherwise.

The New Testament implies that filling the earth is not God's main aim; redeeming it is. He wants to fill the earth with His glory, with the knowledge of His salvation. That is often done through the work of people who remain single.

Jesus—who remained single Himself—speaks of those who "have renounced marriage because of the kingdom of heaven" (Mt. 19:12). Paul says, "It is good for a man not to marry" (1 Cor. 7:1). Was there suddenly something evil about marriage? No. But in those critical times it was better to devote oneself wholly to the work of God's Kingdom.

This is the gardening that needs to be done now: planting the seeds of the Gospel, watering the growing souls, awaiting the harvest. Of course the ordering of creation remains a valid task—the work of artists, engineers, and farmers in their separate ways. By carrying out this work, we are "suitable helpers" with each other. And thus we all—married or single, with children or not—are part of the "very good" creation, made in God's image.

Singles and the Image of God

Some have said that the image of God can only be seen in a male-female combination. The Bible does declare, "So God created man in his own image, in the image of God he created him; male and female he created them" (Gen. 1:27). Does this mean one must be married to fully reflect God's image?

There are many theories about what the image of God means. One holds that the mystery of marriage—two becoming one flesh—mirrors the mystery of the Trinity (Three in One). Another asserts that there is something corresponding to "male and female" in God's nature. Whether or not these are correct, there is a "practical" explanation that seems to make sense—and does not necessarily rule out the others. This view maintains that the "image of God" refers to His role as Creator and as Authority over His creation. He created humanity with the ability, the urge, and the command to continue the creative process.

What does that mean for single people, who cannot righteously procreate? It means that they should express their creativity in other ways. They should build others up and make beautiful, artistic creations and share the redemptive Gospel of Christ with other people. Married people should share in these tasks as well. There is much work to do in the "garden"!

This is not meant to demean the mystery of marriage. God does give us pictures of Himself in that institution. But the beauty of being made good, in God's image, does not require that we join with another in marriage. It rests in the fact that we are commissioned to work creatively with others in God's garden.

Married or Single: Which Is Better?

Why did God create human beings? The Westminster Shorter Catechism says, "To glorify God and enjoy Him forever." Seeing it more from God's perspective, we might say, "To bring enjoyment to God forever." It pleased God to make us, and that remains our highest calling: to please Him.

That's hard to remember in an age of self-fulfillment. The world insists that we please ourselves, that we do "whatever turns us on." But the Bible maintains that our purpose—and the way we function best—is to seek God's pleasure, not our own.

Here single people can have an advantage. Their lack of commitment to a spouse can be turned into an opportunity to be wholly committed to God. Paul states this in 1 Corinthians 7. There's nothing wrong with marital commitment, as Paul clearly teaches; it's just that a single person is freer to seek God's pleasure.

Paul was writing in a time of great immorality and great urgency: "This world in its present form is passing away" (vs. 31). Because of the temptations of immorality, Paul recognized that it was important for some to marry. Marriage is a gift from God, he implies in verse 7. But the ability to stay single, chastely, is also a gift, one preferred by Paul: "It is good for [the unmarried and widows] to stay unmarried, as I am. But if they cannot control themselves, they should marry, for it is better to marry than to burn with passion" (vss. 8, 9).

It was not unusual in Paul's day for religious leaders to forbid marriage. Despite the immorality of the day, there were legalistic, gnostic sects that tried to win their way into the spirit world by shunning all matters of the flesh. This is the "Touch not, taste not, handle not" club Paul opposes in Colossians. In I Timothy, Paul warns against latter-day "hypocritical liars" (4:2) who "forbid people to marry and order them to abstain from certain foods, which God created to be received with thanksgiving by those who believe and who know the truth" (4:3).

Still, Paul prefers that people remain single. Why? "The time is short" (I Cor. 7:29). Nineteen centuries later, we should still have that feeling. We are that much closer to Christ's Second

Coming. That means we mustn't settle in. We are pilgrims; it does not make sense to develop too many attachments to the things of this world. We must devote ourselves thoroughly to the expansion of God's Kingdom.

In this light, Paul's preference becomes clearer. "I would like you to be free from concern. An unmarried man is concerned about the Lord's affairs—how he can please the Lord. But a married man is concerned about the affairs of this world—how he can please his wife—and his interests are divided. An unmarried woman or virgin is concerned about the Lord's affairs: Her aim is to be devoted to the Lord in both body and spirit. But a married woman is concerned about the affairs of this world—how she can please her husband. I am saying this for your own good, not to restrict you, but that you may live in a right way in undivided devotion to the Lord" (I Cor. 7:32-35).

Thus, even though Paul speaks highly of marriage, he presents singleness as a preferred option. "So then, he who marries the virgin does right, but he who does not marry her does even better" (7:38). It is possible to please the Lord and be married, but it is more difficult: "Those who marry will face many troubles in this life, and I want to spare you this" (7:28). Singleness is "better," in a practical sense, because it makes it easier to please God and to do His work, especially in critical times.

Called to Be Single?

People sometimes talk about a special "calling" to singleness. Some are sure they will never marry. Some have promised God they will never marry. In a way, they have "married" God and vowed to be ever faithful.

As God called Moses to lead Israel, Isaiah to prophesy, Paul to travel to Macedonia, or William Carey to go to India, so He has called some people to devote their lives to Him in singleness. But most of us are not like that; we have not heard a special calling.

Most single people just don't know whether they will marry. So far in their lives, their day-by-day efforts to answer the general call of God (to please Him) have not led to marriage. Maybe someday it will happen; maybe not.

Are these single Christians "called" to be single? Yes! They are called to be single *today.* Tomorrow God may call them to marry. They need to stay sensitive to God's leading each day, and to be content wherever that leading takes them.

Kevin is a 29-year-old single person. He's worried because he has never felt "called" to be single. He comes to you with his concern. How can you help?

You can encourage him to relax. You can let him know that we are all called to please God in whatever state we find ourselves. If God has not indicated that it pleases Him for Kevin to marry, then God is "calling" Kevin to please Him in singleness.

But what if God wanted Kevin to marry at one time and Kevin blew it? God's desire that Kevin please Him today remains in force. If there was sin involved in that previous situation, Kevin should confess it to God, who forgives. If restitution is necessary, Kevin should see what he can do. He is not necessarily "doomed" to be single forever or always wander apart from God's will. God's mercies are "new every morning" (Lam. 3:23).

But how can a person know whether God wants him or her to get married? In his book *Decision-Making and the Will of God: A Biblical Alternative to the Traditional View,* Garry Friesen says you have to start with Scripture. "In those areas specifically addressed by the Bible, the revealed commands and principles of God (His moral will) are to be obeyed." But there are many areas of life that the Bible does not directly address—such as what person to marry, what job to take, etc. In these matters "the believer is free and responsible to choose his own course of action," provided it is within the attitude and behavior guidelines of God's moral will.

In such decisions, writes Friesen, "the objective of the Christian is to make wise decisions on the basis of spiritual expediency." Friesen points out the many times in the New Testament when church leaders began their announcements of decisions with the statement, "It seemed good to us. . . ." Through Bible study and prayer, with godly attitudes and wise counsel, these early church leaders did what they thought was best for the Kingdom of God.

Similarly, the Lord will help us know what pleases Him if we stay tuned to Him. The decisions of whether or not to marry, and whom to marry, can be made with confidence if we are seeking His wisdom.[1]

A Theology of Single Sexuality

As Scripture attests, there is a wide range of "fleshly" behavior (Gal. 5:19-21). The "lusts of the flesh" are not limited to sexual immorality. But in the lives of most single people, sexual issues are of crucial importance—especially in our sex-crazy world.

Paul's discussion of the Spirit and the flesh (Rom. 8, Eph. 6) gives us a helpful image. It helps us understand the battle waged daily over our souls. It's hard to win a battle of body vs. spirit, because we are body *and* spirit. No matter which side wins that battle, we seem to lose. But when we see the struggle occurring between the spiritual forces of life and death, it's no contest.

It's not always easy to see these things clearly, however. That's partly because we are being lied to. Fleming Rutledge of Grace Church in New York City says it simply: "Canaan tells lies." Canaan is her term for the world around us. Israel had idol-worshiping neighbors in Canaan; so do we, except that our neighbors worship money and sex. They tell "very convincing and seductive lies," Rutledge says. "A system of lies not only deceives, but also destroys."[2]

The world says sex will set people free; that's a lie. Out of its proper marital context, sexual activity enslaves. The world says people are only as masculine or feminine as their last sexual experience indicates; that's a lie. The world says people's physical need for sex is just too strong to resist; that's a lie.

As Wesley W. Nelson writes in *Liberation* (Covenant Press, 1974), "The biological sex drive is not nearly the overwhelming urge it appears to be. . . . It is when sexual attraction becomes associated with acceptance and when a person's self-image becomes dependent on sexual adequacy that the desire for sex becomes escalated far beyond the biological urge itself."

Single people are misguided if they blame God for giving them such a strong sex drive without permission to satisfy it. The problem seems to be not so much in the way humans are made, but in the whispers of Canaan, which go something like this: "You are not worth much if you're not sexy."

Inner-city pastor Tom Goodhue wrote in *His* magazine (January, 1983), "We are battling not only against the urges of our own flesh, but also against social forces which encourage lust." Paul put it similarly in Ephesians 6:12: "For our struggle is not against flesh and blood, but against the rulers, against the authorities, against the powers of this dark world and against the spiritual forces of evil in the heavenly realms.''

One of the greatest lies told today is that we can attain satisfaction by divorcing body from spirit and engaging in purely physical pleasure. ''Whatever feels good, do it,'' people say, ignoring any spiritual implications. Having sex—with another, with oneself, with an image in a movie or a magazine—is purely physical, they say, and pleasurable for that reason. ''As long as it doesn't hurt anybody, it's okay. After all, it's your body. Do what you want with it.''

No matter what Canaan says, the things we do with our bodies have spiritual implications. Promiscuity and pornography may not always visibly hurt people, but they are sins of emptiness, sins of separation. Sexual intercourse without the commitment of marriage separates the physical pleasure from the spiritual sustenance that should make sex truly pleasurable. Becoming enslaved by habitual fantasy or masturbation means playing dead, spiritually speaking. It means saying, ''My body is just a body. It knows what it wants. No need for spiritual control.''

The Corinthians had a saying: ''Food for the stomach and the stomach for food.'' The saying was really about sex, at least as Paul quotes it in I Corinthians 6; it implies that sex is the only reason for us to have bodies. But Paul turned it around: ''The body is not meant for sexual immorality, but for the Lord, and the Lord for the body. By his power God raised the Lord from the dead, and he will raise us also'' (1 Cor. 6:13, 14).

Because of the Resurrection, our bodies have a higher purpose than just pleasure. Because of the Resurrection, we have the power to shun immorality, and we have the life of God's Spirit available to us. Why should we keep playing dead? Promiscuity, pornography, and masturbation are deeds of death—because they treat the body as though it were just a hunk of spiritless flesh.

''Count yourselves dead to sin but alive to God in Christ Jesus,'' Paul wrote to the Romans. ''Therefore do not let sin reign in your mortal body so that you obey its evil desires. Do not offer the parts of your body to sin, as instruments of wickedness, but rather offer yourselves to God, as those who have been brought from death to life; and offer the parts of your body to him as instruments of righteousness. For sin shall not be your master'' (Rom. 6:11-14).

"But wait," says Roger, a 31-year-old single man. "I agree that promiscuity is bad. Sex without love is pointless. I believe in sex with love, and I love my girlfriend. What's wrong with us having sex?"

This is yet another lie Canaan tells, but it is far more subtle because it sounds so good. We might call it "The Ethic of Intimacy." Tim Stafford calls it exactly that in a January 16, 1987 article in *Christianity Today.* Stafford lists the tenets of this new ethic: Sex within intimacy is good, whether or not you're married; in a relationship, both individuals are independent; intimacy is based on personal compatibility; sex is a private matter; sex has no necessary consequences (you will have good experiences and bad experiences, but you can always move on); there should be no double standard (women should have the same rights in relationships as men); sex requires maturity (since sexual decisions are based on situational ethics, it takes adult wisdom to deal with them).

The Ethic of Intimacy does not oppose marriage. But the pattern is (a) sleep with someone if you really like him or her; (b) live together for a while; and (c) if things work out, get married.

What's wrong with that? In his article Stafford says it well: "Christians can hardly be against intimacy. We want it, too. What we must say, I think, is that the Ethic of Intimacy is too weak—too weak to deal with the powerful human urges, often destructive, always potential, that make up our sexuality. It is like walking a lion on a leash. Sometimes he goes where you want him to. Sometimes he will not. Sometimes he turns around and devours you.

"The Ethic of Intimacy is inherently vague; under sway of emotions you can convince yourself anything is intimate. And there is a strange current of passivity and fatalism in it—a surrendering of self to the gods of eros—which undermines human dignity. . . .The Christian ideal places a person's will (not emotions) at the center: Love is work to be done, and intimacy is to be created through persistent self-sacrifice. . . .

"Christians have another concern. A pure and loving monogamy reflects a pure love of God. As Paul tells us, husband and wife are like Christ and His church. We must train ourselves to be monogamous both with our spouse and with our Lord. If we lose this singularity in marriage, we will at the least lose a way of understanding our relationship with God."[3]

Redemption: Hope for Singles

What hope can our "theology of singleness" offer hurting single people? Are they to rely on their own efforts to overcome low self-image, establish a relationship with God, and battle temptation?

No. In our discussions with single people in crisis we must always help them to see the Good News of redemption. Sin destroys relationships, distorts self-image, skews sexuality, and obscures the purpose of life—but God offers redemption through Jesus Christ. Through His sacrificial death, atonement was made, and humanity began to be restored.

Jesus restores our self-image, because He puts the focus on Himself. We can look in the mirror and see Jesus, figuratively speaking, because He takes our place before the Father. We are being conformed to Christ's image (Rom. 8:29).

Jesus restores our sense of purpose, making it possible for us to please the Father. Twice during Jesus' ministry, the Father announced, "This is my Son, whom I love; with him I am well pleased" (Mt. 3:17; 17:5). The Son was perfectly fulfilling humanity's purpose—to please God. In His power, we can follow the same calling.

Jesus also gives us access to the power which allows us to obey—to be faithful sexually as well as in other areas. Through Him we are indwelt by the Holy Spirit, the One who comforts us and oversees our transformation into the kinds of people He wants us to be.

Jesus brought meaning to the mystery of marriage by taking the Church as His Bride. In Him male and female, single and married, can live side by side—in His peace.

Involving the Church

A synagogue in Manhattan emphasizes outreach to single people. Its members affectionately call it the "Wink and Stare" synagogue. "It's a much more civilized place to meet than in a singles' bar," comments a 28-year-old woman, noting that most men use their "opening line" to wish her a good Sabbath. "On Friday nights I know that other people are out on Columbus Avenue looking for Mr. Goodbar," she says. "I've got someplace better to go."[1]

Similarly, more and more Christian churches are positioning themselves as places for single people to meet. Churches can help meet single people's needs for connection and companionship far better than singles bars do. Churches can also help meet a host of spiritual needs. But they should do this with care, lest the church scene become as dehumanizing as the bar scene.

So how should churches reach out to single people?

Proper outreach happens at the official, whole-church level; at the unofficial, individual and family level; and at the singles group level. Launching a singles group is fine, but ministry to single people should not end there. This ministry needs to belong to your whole church.

The Whole Church

Helping single people doesn't have to be *the* priority in every local church; after all, there are many areas in which the church needs to minister. But singles ministry should not be neglected. Here are seven suggestions for church leaders who want to develop a church environment in which many singleness crises can be overcome and even avoided.

1. *Develop a working theology of singleness.*

See the previous chapter for ideas. As you proceed, you may want to ask yourself questions like these:

- If marriage is good, is singleness bad?
- Does a single person have less of a relationship with God than

a married person? Does he or she have a more spiritual one?
- Is a single person "half" a person, incomplete, unfulfilled?
- Is a single person less equipped to minister in the church than a married person is?
- Does God prohibit single people from taking certain offices in the church?

Once church leaders have considered questions like these, the results can be passed on to the entire congregation.

2. *Acknowledge single people in your church program.*

Sermons about motherhood, fatherhood, marriage, and family are important. But how often do most congregations hear about the single life, the courage it takes to accept singleness, or choosing singleness as a means of service? Perhaps not often enough.

It's not too hard to spot some actions that leave out single people—for example, inviting the congregation to come to a church dinner with "a dish large enough for your family and two others." It's more difficult to notice subtler actions and attitudes that may cause single people to feel left out. For example, many churches recognize marriages and births—but never the milestones in single people's lives—from the pulpit. A sensitive pastor could help by asking a single person in the church to alert him when he says something that offends or neglects single people.

3. *Listen to single people.*

What do single people in your church think, feel, and need? Would it be helpful to invite some of them to address the church board on this subject?

How about dialogue among single and married people in the congregation? An evening set aside for this purpose could enhance fellowship and educate both "sides" as well. Some single people assume those who are married never feel lonely or afraid; some married people assume "singles" lead glamorous, exciting lives and have lots of spending money. Discussion might dispel some myths and pave the way for more honest friendships. It might also keep single people from jumping into unwise marriages in search of ideal wedded bliss, or married people from choosing divorce for the sake of an ideal "freedom".

4. *Consider single people for leadership positions.*

You may or may not want to follow the lead of one Illinois church which appointed single adults to all its boards and committees. One author, Nicholas B. Christoff, even suggests a quota system to "facilitate the return of alienated single adults" to the church. He writes, "Require that at least one-third of your church council or governing board be single men or women."[2] His quota is based on the fact that roughly a third of U.S. adults are single, but ignores other important considerations.

You may find it helpful to ask yourself questions like these:

- How many of the adults in our church are single? How many on the boards and committees of our church are single? If there is a great difference between those two percentages, is it time for some "affirmative action"?
- If our church has a married person as senior pastor, should we make a point of adding a single person to the pastoral staff at the next opportunity?

5. *Use the gifts and talents of single people.*

Single people should be servants as well as leaders in the church. But the gifts of many single people are underused. Why?

The "spouse factor" is one cause. One married man received an honorary doctorate, but didn't tell anyone at church because he was so humble. After several weeks his wife quietly let the pastor know, and the pastor put a note in the bulletin. It was proper for the man's brothers and sisters to commend him on his honor. But if he were single, it would never have happened.

Ever hear a spouse say, "Did you know my wife plays piano?" or, "My husband would love to teach the adult class"? Single people don't have this public relations department. Spouses may also encourage each other to use their gifts: "Go ahead, honey, you can do it," or, "Maybe you should volunteer for that." Single people often lack this extra motivation.

Church leaders can overcome this problem by getting to know the single people of the church and learning what their gifts are. Congregations can be encouraged to do the same, and to become each other's motivators as appropriate.

Lack of commitment is another problem when it comes to the use of some single people's gifts in the church. "You can't really count on single people, can you?" a choir director might ask. "They're always changing their plans, traveling on weekends, losing interest, moving, or even getting married." This is one stereotype that's often true, especially for younger single people.

In the short run, however, single people may be the most faithful servants of the church. A single person might not sign on to teach the second-grade Sunday School class for the next ten years, but he or she may stay up all night completing a multimedia worship presentation or sitting with a seriously ill parishioner. "Their willingness to work makes up for their lack of [long-range] commitment," one singles pastor told us.

But note that a lack of long-range commitment is not a trait of all single people. Many, especially as they grow older, become just as dependable as stable married people, perhaps more so. In fact, one large church in Pennsylvania found that 25 percent of its ministries were headed by single people.

6. *Define your church's view of divorce and communicate that clearly to the congregation.*

Divorced people make up a significant percentage of the single population in many churches. Do these single people, many of whom face crises, know how your church feels about them?

One divorced woman with a lovely voice and many other talents had to remain on the sidelines. When she talked with the pastor about singing in a service, he said that might be possible. But she would not be allowed to sing bright, happy songs, he said, since that might indicate that being divorced is a blessed state. That was the only position on divorce she had heard her church take. She would have been happy to live within her church's guidelines—if only she knew what they were.

7. *Plan activities that mix single and married, younger and older.*

A nurse from Minnesota confessed that she looked for a church *without* a separate singles ministry—because the church she had been attending had a "massive singles group" into which "every single was slotted whether you liked it or not."

There are valid reasons for grouping people according to age, interests, and marital status—for some activities. But people of all ages and life stages need to fellowship with and learn from each other, too. Try planning some activities that intentionally mix ages and life stages. Single people and young marrieds might go bowling together, for example; a potluck could feature assigned seating that mixes ages and marital status.

Sessions for Church Leaders

To discuss your church's ministry to single people, you may wish to schedule a series of meetings for church leaders. Here are ideas for four such sessions:

Session 1: Introduction

Read and discuss Genesis 1-3 and I Corinthians 7. What Biblical principles about single people and the church can you draw from these passages and others? Appoint one or two people to summarize your conclusions in writing. Review what your church is already doing for single people, especially for those in crisis.

Session 2: Fact-finding

Invite two or three single people from your church to address the group, seeking to answer questions like these: What problems do single people in your congregation face? When do they feel neglected? What programs for singles are working? What changes can they suggest?

Session 3: Discussion

Discuss and approve a written statement on single people and your church, including the role of single people in leadership. Discuss the concerns and ideas your guests presented in the last session.

Session 4: Action

Decide what actions you can take in the following areas:

- Asking one or two single people to monitor the church program for ''singles neglect'' during the next year;
- Identifying the gifts of single people in your church and encouraging their use;
- Appointing more single people to positions of leadership;
- Starting a specific ''singles ministry'' if your church has none;
- Scheduling activities which mix single and married people;
- Clarifying your church's position on how to treat divorced people;
- Publicizing help available to single people who face crises; and
- Discussing these issues further as needed.

Congregational Awareness

Every person in your congregation can participate in ministry to hurting single people. You can help the process along by communicating the following hints.

1. *Get to know single people individually.* Each one is unique, with unique needs and gifts to offer. Don't assume that all single people are desperate for marriage, rich, poor, living in the fast lane, defective, selfish, irresponsible, or burdened with too much free time.

2. *Respect the privacy of single people, but be ready to help those you've come to know.* Many single people have a strong sense of privacy. They are also used to putting on a face that says, "Everything's under control"—even when it isn't. Some find close friends to confide in, as a married person might with a spouse, but many don't. Show your concern, but don't dig unless you've earned the right.

3. *Recognize the family needs of single people.* Many families can count on their own little communities of understanding people. Some single people set up their own makeshift "families" in an effort to meet this need, but many don't. Young singles particularly need families; often they are just starting out on their own, having moved to a new area or a new job.

If you're part of a family unit, welcome a single person into your midst. Offer hospitality; be there when she or he needs to borrow a hammer, do laundry, recover from an illness, get a ride to the airport, or just be with someone. Remember that, as one survey found, the loneliest times for single people tend to be holidays, birthdays, and Sunday afternoons.[3]

A caution: Some single people tend not to return favors and invitations. This is probably more true of men than women, younger than older. It may not be easy to keep helping those who seem unconcerned with such courtesies, but try to remember that they, too, need God's kind of unconditional love.

4. *Affirm Biblical principles of sexuality.* Many who rail against the world's preoccupation with "sex appeal" still "ooh" and "ah" when a young man brings an attractive girlfriend to church. This may lead single people to think they're worth more if they date attractive people. It's hard enough to deal with low self-image, high expectations, and temptation without having to fight them in church, too. Try to help single people look beyond glamor and treasure the beauty of the soul.

Similarly, when two single people of opposite sexes have a close friendship, don't assume it's a romance or try to push them into marriage. Single people, like everyone else, need those who are "just friends."

To help members of the congregation understand and support single people, you may want to hold a series of "awareness meetings" in addition to dealing with the topic in sermons. These meetings could be incorporated into Sunday evening services or adult Sunday School classes—any setting in which open discussion is encouraged. Here are suggested outlines for three such meetings.

Meeting 1: What Does the Bible Say?

To examine singleness from God's perspective, study I Corinthians 7 and Genesis 1, 2. Discuss: Are singleness and marriage both good options for God's people? What are the advantages of each? Do Paul's recommendations on singleness and marriage apply today? What does the Creation account tell us about singleness and marriage?

Use this book as a resource as you discuss the worthiness of both singleness and marriage. Have students share examples of ways in which their marital status has enabled them to serve God—or made it difficult to do so.

Close this meeting, as well as the next two, by having married and single people pray in small groups for each other's needs.

Meeting 2: Listening to Each Other

Read Ephesians 4:1-16 and Colossians 3:12-17. Talk about the attitudes God wants us to have toward each other in the church. Emphasize the unity of the Body, diverse as its members may be.

Distribute pencils and paper. Ask single people to complete the following sentences:

Married people are . . . .
It bothers me when married people . . . .
Sometimes I wish I was married because . . . .
The best thing about being single is . . . .
The worst thing about being single is . . . .

Have married people complete similar sentences, but with the marital status reversed ("It bothers me when single people . . . ."). Then discuss answers, encouraging compassion for one another. If your group is too large, appoint panels of married and single people to discuss issues raised by the sentence completion.

Meeting 3: Helping Each Other

Read Philippians 2:1-11. Discuss how this passage can influence the way single and married people treat one another. If the leaders of your church have already composed a statement on the church's attitude toward single people, present it to the group.

Divide into small groups which contain both married and single people. Have them discuss these questions:

- How can I as a single/married person help you as a married/single person?
- How can I help you serve God more effectively?
- How can we get to know each other better?
- How can I allow you to help me?
- What would you like to see our church do for you?
- What would you like to do for our church?

Ask each group to write down its ideas and turn them in for consideration by church leaders. If possible, follow up in a month or two with a social event attended by both married and single people.

The Singles Group

The singles ministry movement has been booming for several years, and for good reasons. You may find it helpful to start one in your church if you haven't already. Keep the following points in mind, however.

1. Don't start a singles ministry just because other churches are doing it, or because it will boost your attendance, or because it will give your church a young, cutting-edge image. *Do* start a singles ministry because you see needs among the single people in your church and community that can best be met with this sort of programming. Be sure you have the support of your church leadership; without it, says one successful singles pastor, "you can forget the whole thing."

2. Find a core group among your single people. No matter how dynamic a singles group leader may be, you need to start with at least three or four. A singles group is primarily a social organism, even though it does more than enjoy social activities. Your core people are probably the ones who will follow up visitors, organize programs, do some lay counseling, and pray.

Don't seek only "beautiful people" for your core group, hoping they will attract others. That may build your numbers quickly, but your ministry may be only skin deep. It would be far better for your group to become known as one that welcomes single people regardless of physical appeal, and that helps them attain the beauty of Christlikeness.

3. Find the right meeting place, one in which single people will feel comfortable. One pastor says the location must be "culturally relevant," and for singles that may not be in the church building. Try for a place that's large enough for your

group, but not so large that it makes the group seem small.

4. Keep having fun, even if only a few people show up. Don't be too disappointed by small attendance. Try to plan activities that can be enjoyed by four or forty, and have a blast doing them. Your enthusiasm will probably attract others, though it may happen slowly. Whether or not your group grows numerically, focus on ministry to individuals, not crowds.

5. Band together with other churches. Writing of singles ministries, Joseph Bayly observed, "Healthy programs tend to flourish in larger-than-average churches. As an alternative, groups from several churches could combine their membership for one ministry, since a 'critical mass' is needed to achieve the best results."

That is especially true when one of the reasons for attending such a group is to find dates or mates. The possibilities of finding a friend or a true love are greater when two or more groups merge for certain social activities.

6. Accept the fact that single people from your church may want to attend groups at other churches. If your group is small, you may lose some who like the excitement and increased social contacts of large groups. Try to keep in touch with these people; huge groups can provide excitement but sometimes lack personal ministry. If you maintain caring contact with a single person who has left your group for "greener" pastures, he or she may seek you out when crisis comes.

7. Get help from the married as well as the single. At least one singles pastor involved in national leadership believes singles ministries need the involvement of married couples. In his church a childless man and wife in their 60s developed a "real heart for singles," and became so involved that they made friends only among the singles. "They knew that once they started the dinner party routine they'd never have time for the ministry. We could not do a lot of what we do," the pastor says, "if it wasn't for them."

8. Don't neglect Bible study and discipleship. Single people need solid spiritual nourishment as they face temptation, make crucial decisions, and question their spiritual roots. Bible study will not be as popular as social activities, but it will help those who attend to deal with their crises and those of their friends.

Single people can be further strengthened as they teach and serve. "The idea is to funnel people into service opportunities as quickly as possible,'' says one singles pastor. In his church, 35 to 40 percent of outreach ministries are performed by single people.

9. Develop spiritual accountability. Single people tend to ''float free,'' not having to answer to anyone for their personal lives or spiritual growth. Can you set up groups of two or three to pray regularly and to study the Bible apart from the whole-group program?

10. Be sensitive to spiritual searching. Many who marry and have children feel the need to ''settle down'' spiritually. They cast their lot with the church and grow within it. But during their singlehood, they may remain on the fringe.

Love these searchers. Challenge them, but affirm their desire to know God. Trim your faith to the essentials as you communicate it to them. Keep the focus on Jesus Christ. Pray for and with them.

11. Don't ignore the big topics: sex and money. Both can be difficult to discuss, but they are critical for the single person. Discuss ways in which the world tempts us; talk about strategies for overcoming temptation. Offer God's forgiveness for sin and claim His power to start anew in righteousness.

Will You Help?

You don't have to set up an impressive program to start ministering to single people who hurt. All you need to begin are access to God's power through His Son, Jesus Christ; a servant's heart; and at least one single person who needs to be served.

Look around next Sunday morning. Is it possible that some single people in your church feel invisible as they sit in their pews? Are some of them facing crises of loneliness, doubt, bitterness, or entrapment in sin? Do others long to serve God by using their gifts in your fellowship, but don't know how to get involved?

Because you care, you can help. Through listening and counsel, careful interpretation of Scripture, nurturing a caring church environment, and just plain ''being there'' for single people who hurt, you can guide them through the silent but significant crises of singleness.

Notes

Introduction

1. Margaret Clarkson, ''Singleness: His Share for Me,'' *Christianity Today,* February 16, 1979, p. 15.
2. Paul Welter, *How to Help a Friend* (Wheaton, Ill.: Tyndale House Publishers, 1978), p. 19).

Chapter One

1. Census figures cited from *The World Almanac 1987* (New York: Pharos Books). ''Singles'' include divorced and widowed.
2. *The New York Times,* November 20, 1985.
3. *The New York Times,* November 6, 1986.
4. Leonard Cargan and Matthew Melko, *Singles: Myths and Realities* (Beverly Hills, CA: Sage Publications, 1982), pp. 37-41.
5. *The New York Times,* November 20, 1985, and September 16, 1985.
6. Tim Stafford, ''Intimacy: Our Latest Sexual Fantasy,'' *Christianity Today,* January 16, 1987, p. 22.
7. Cargan and Melko, p. 42.
8. *The World Almanac 1987,* p. 775.
9. Merle Shain, *Some Men Are More Perfect Than Others* (New York: Charterhouse Press, 1973), p. 27.
10. Jacqueline Simenauer and David Carroll, *Singles: The New Americans* (New York: Simon & Schuster, 1982), pp. 20-31.
11. Jeffrey Ullman, *The Singles Almanac* (New York: World Almanac Publications, 1986), p. 21.
12. Aaron Hass, *Love, Sex and the Single Man* (New York: Franklin Watts, 1983).

Chapter Three

1. Paul Welter, *How to Help a Friend* (Wheaton, Ill.: Tyndale House Publishers, 1978), pp. 71-77.
2. Welter, pp. 88, 89.

Chapter Five

1. Walter Trobisch, *U,* February, 1987, p.6.
2. Janice Harayda, *The Joy of Being Single* (New York: Doubleday, 1986), p. 11.
3. Randy C. Alcorn, *Christians in the Wake of the Sexual Revolution* (Portland, Ore.: Multnomah Press, 1985), p. 220.
4. Walter and Ingrid Trobisch, *My Beautiful Feeling* (Downers Grove, Ill.: InterVarsity Press, 1976), p. 65.

Chapter Six

1. Garry Friesen and J. Robin Maxson, *Decision-Making and the Will of God* (Portland, Ore.: Multnomah Press, 1980).
2. The material from Fleming Rutledge comes from talks she gave at Grace Church in New York City in 1982.
3. Tim Stafford, "Intimacy: Our Latest Sexual Fantasy," *Christianity Today,* January 16, 1987, pp. 21-27.

Chapter Seven

1. Peter Kerr, "Singles Seek Social Life at Houses of Worship," *The New York Times,* April 1, 1985, p. B2.
2. Nicholas Christoff, *Saturday Night, Sunday Morning: Singles and the Church* (San Francisco: Harper and Row, 1978), p. 115.
3. Joseph Bayly, "Saved, Single, and Second-Class," *Eternity,* March, 1983, p. 24.

Bibliography

Counseling

Collins, Gary R., 1980. *Christian Counseling: A Comprehensive Guide*. Waco, Tex.: Word, Inc. Designed to assist pastors and leaders in their day-to-day ministries; includes an overview and chapters on specific problems. Also 1976, *How to Be a People Helper.* Santa Ana, Calif.: Vision House Publishers. More methods from the expert counselor.

Collins, Gary R., ed., 1986. Resources for Christian Counseling series. Waco, Tex.: Word, Inc. Included in the series are:

Collins, Gary R. *Innovative Approaches to Counseling;*
Hart, Archibald D. *Counseling the Depressed*;
McBurney, Louis. *Counseling Christian Workers;*
Swihart, Judson and Richardson, Gerald. *Crisis Counseling;*
Walters, Richard P. *Counseling and Lack of Self-Control;*
Wilson, Earl. *Counseling and Guilt;*
Wright, H. Norman. *Self-Talk, Imagery, and Prayer in Counseling*.

Crabb, Lawrence J., Jr., 1977. *Effective Biblical Counseling: A Model for Helping Caring Christians Become Capable Counselors*. Grand Rapids: Zondervan. Crabb has become an influential leader in Christian counseling, and with good reason.

Crabb, Lawrence J., Jr. and Allender, Dan B., 1984. *Encouragement: The Key to Caring*. Grand Rapids: Zondervan. A topic that is essential to a good singles ministry.

McKenna, David. *The Psychology of Jesus: The Dynamics of Christian Wholeness*. Waco, Tex.: Word, Inc. A study of the psychology, personality, and practice of Jesus, the model for fulfilling personhood.

Oates, Wayne E. *The Presence of God in Pastoral Counseling*. Waco, Tex.: Word, Inc. The theory and technique of going beyond mere counseling to communicating the presence of God.

Shelley, Marshall, 1986. *Helping Those Who Don't Want Help*. Waco, Tex.: Word, Inc. Solving the problem of dealing with those who think they have no problem.

Welter, Paul 1978. *How to Help a Friend*. Wheaton, Ill.: Tyndale House Publishers. Immensely helpful, practical guide to lay counseling.

Dating, Friendship, Marriage

Augsburger, David. *Caring Enough to Confront: How to Understand and Express Your Deepest Feelings Toward Others*. Scottdale, Pa.: Herald Press, 1980. *Caring Enough to Forgive/Not Forgive*. Herald Press, 1981. *Caring Enough to Hear and Be Heard*. Herald Press, 1982. *When Caring Is Not Enough*. Herald Press, 1983. These books are enormously helpful.

Howard, J. Grant, 1979. *The Trauma of Transparency: A Biblical Approach to Inter-Personal Communication*. Portland, Ore.: Multnomah Press.

Huggett, Joyce,1985. *Dating, Sex and Friendship*. Downers Grove, Ill.: InterVarsity Press. Good advice from a woman's perspective, but not just for women.

Kirby, Scott, 1982. *Dating: Guidelines from the Bible*. Grand Rapids: Baker Book House. A conservative look.

Lewis, C.S., 1960. *The Four Loves*. New York: Harcourt Brace Jovanovich, Inc. A simple, eloquent, classic discussion of four kinds of human relations. His chapter on friendship will revolutionize your concept.

McGinnis, Alan L., 1979. *The Friendship Factor.* Minneapolis: Augsburg. Also 1983, *The Romance Factor.* New York: Harper & Row.

Rinehart, Stacy and Paula, 1983. *Choices: Finding God's Way in Dating, Sex, Singleness and Marriage*. Colorado Springs: NavPress.

Guidance, Decision Making

Ferguson, Sinclair B, 1981. *Discovering God's Will*. Carlisle, Pa.: Banner of Truth, 1981. A classic Reformed view of God's guidance in big decisions and in daily life. Ferguson presents good theology in a devotional style.

Friesen, Garry and Maxson, J. Robin, 1981. *Decision-Making and the Will of God: A Biblical Alternative to the Traditional View* (expanded edition). Portland, Ore.: Multnomah Press. A book that caused quite a ruffle among evangelicals when it was released. Challenges the notion that God has one mate, school, or job in mind for you. Presents the freedom of sensible decision making within Biblical guidelines.

Smedes, Lewis B, 1986. *Choices: Making Right Decisions in a Complex World*. New York: Harper & Row, 1986. Guidelines based on moral standards and how to apply them to real life.

Personal Development

Baker, Don and Nester, Emery, 1983. *Depression: Finding Hope & Meaning in Life's Darkest Shadow.* Portland, Ore.: Multnomah Press.

Carter, W. Leslie, et al, 1982. *Why Be Lonely? A Guide to Meaningful Relationships*. Grand Rapids: Baker Book House. Christian counselors and psychiatrists analyze the causes and cures.

Conway, Jim, 1978. *Men in Mid-Life Crisis*. Elgin, Ill.: David C. Cook Publishing Co. One-of-a-kind book; very practical.

Conway, Jim and Conway, Sally, 1983. *Women in Mid-Life Crisis*. Wheaton, Ill.: Tyndale House Publishers. The sequel.

Cosgrove, Mark P. *The Amazing Body Human: God's Design for Personhood*. Grand Rapids: Baker Book House. The uniqueness of the human body as evidence of God's design for us as persons.

Huggett, Joyce, 1985. *Creative Conflict*. Downers Grove, Ill.: InterVarsity Press.

Kreeft, Peter, 1986. *Making Sense Out of Suffering*. Ann Arbor, Mich.: Servant Books. Eloquent, rational, and compelling; this philosopher writes as clearly and warmly as C.S. Lewis. Highly recommended.

Lutzer, Erwin W., 1983. *Managing Your Emotions*. Wheaton, Ill.: Victor Books.

Swindoll, Charles R. *Dropping Your Guard*. Waco, Tex.: Word, Inc.. Focuses on the needs and joys of honestly facing people without our masks, especially in the church.

Timmons, Tim, 1983. *Loneliness Is Not a Disease*. New York: Ballantine Books. Helpful discussion in sermon/pep talk style.

Tournier, Paul 1962. *Escape from Loneliness*. Philadelphia: The Westminster Press. A graceful discussion from a psychiatrist.

White, John, 1982. *The Masks of Melancholy: A Christian Physician Looks at Depression and Suicide*. Downers Grove,

Ill.: InterVarsity Press. He is also a psychiatrist and a wonderfully insightful writer.

Self-Acceptance

Baker, Don, 1985. *Acceptance—Loosing the Webs of Personal Insecurity.* Portland, Ore.: Multnomah Press. A wide look at the question of self-love.

Berry, Jo. *Becoming God's Special Woman—Develop Self-Worth His Way.* Old Tappan, N.J.: Fleming Revell Publishers. Also 1978, *Can You Love Yourself?* Ventura, Calif.: Regal Books.

Birkey, Verna, 1977. *You Are Very Special: A Biblical Guide to Self-Worth.* Old Tappan, N.J.: Fleming Revell Publishers.

Miller, Keith. 1985. *Please Love Me.* Waco., Tex.: Word, Inc. Story of a search for acceptance that ends in discovering Jesus Christ.

Smith, Blaine, 1984. *One of a Kind.* Downers Grove, Ill.: InterVarsity Press. Recommended by many counselors.

Stafford, Tim, 1986. *Do You Sometimes Feel Like a Nobody?* Wheaton, Ill.: Tyndale House Publishers.

Sexual Issues

Alcorn, Randy C., 1985. *Christians in the Wake of the Sexual Revolution.* Portland, Ore.: Multnomah Press. Explores society's pervasive sexual assault and offers steps to sexual sanity.

Elliot, Elisabeth, 1984. *Passion and Purity.* Old Tappan, N.J.: Fleming Revell Co. Personal recollection of her first love relationship.

Lutzer, Erwin, W., 1983. *Living with Your Passions: A Christian's Guide to Sexual Purity.* Wheaton, Ill.: Victor Books. A guide to resisting temptation.

Miles, Herbert J., 1972. *Sexual Understanding Before Marriage.* Grand Rapids: Zondervan. Also *Singles, Sex and Marriage.* Waco, Tex.: Word, Inc.

Penner, Clifford and Penner, Joyce, 1981. *The Gift of Sex.* Waco, Tex.: Word, Inc. A medical, psychological, and spiritual discussion.

Smedes, Lewis B., 1983. *Mere Morality.* Grand Rapids: William B. Eerdmans Publishing Co. In this study of five moral commandments, see chapter on adultery. Also 1976, *Sex for Christians.* Grand Rapids: William B. Eerdmans Publishing Co.

Generally a Christian viewpoint, but noncommittal on essential issues.

Stafford, Tim, 1977. *A Love Story: Questions and Answers on Sex*. Grand Rapids: Zondervan.

Trobisch, Walter, 1979. *Living with Unfulfilled Desires*. Downers Grove, Ill.: InterVarsity Press. Correspondence with high school and college students.

Trobisch, Walter and Trobisch, Ingrid, 1976. *My Beautiful Feeling: Correspondence with Ilona*. Downers Grove, Ill.: InterVarsity Press. A sensitive, factual discussion of masturbation.

Wilson, Earl. 1984. *Sexual Sanity*. Downers Grove, Ill.: InterVarsity Press. Examination of sexual obsessions and how to break them.

White, John, 1977. *Eros Defiled: The Christian and Sexual Sin*. Downers Grove, Ill.: InterVarsity Press. The evangelical psychologist's perceptive analysis.

Singleness

Bence, Evelyn, 1982. *Leaving Home: The Making of an Independent Woman*. Philadelphia: Bridgebooks/The Westminster Press. Journal-like portrait of making hard transitions alone.

Christoff, Nicholas B., 1978. *Saturday Night, Sunday Morning: Singles and the Church*. New York: Harper & Row. Though not from an evangelical perspective, still challenging, with helpful suggestions.

Clarkson, Margaret, 1978. *So You're Single*. Wheaton, Ill.: Harold Shaw Publishers. A classic from an eloquent lady.

Collins, Gary R., ed., 1976. *It's Okay to Be Single*. Waco, Tex.: Word, Inc. Essays by several single evangelicals, on a range of topics.

Evening, Margaret, 1974. *Who Walk Alone*. Downers Grove, Ill.: InterVarsity Press. Feisty, brave, and substantial, by a British missionary.

Karssen, Gien, rev. ed. 1983. *Getting the Most Out of Being Single*. Colorado Springs: NavPress.

Landgraf, John R., 1982. *Creative Singlehood and Pastoral Care*. Philadelphia: Fortress Press. Very helpful, though not all will agree with its theology.

Lyon, William, 1977. *A Pew for One, Please: The Church and the Single Person*. New York: The Seabury Press.

McAllaster, Elva, 1979. *Free to Be Single*. Chappaqua, N.Y.: Christian Herald Books. Like a long, comfortable talk between friends.

Miller, Keith and Miller, Andrea, 1981. *The Single Experience*. Waco, Tex.: Word, Inc.

Simenauer, Jacqueline, and Carroll, David, 1983. *Singles: The New Americans*. New American Library. Based on a national survey of single Americans, it examines practices of dating, mating, and relating.

Taylor, Rhena, 1984. *Single and Whole*. Downers Grove, Ill.: InterVarsity Press. Brief, but intelligent and challenging.

Wood, Britton, 1977. *Single Adults Want to Be the Church Too*. Nashville, Tenn.: Broadman Press.